Dear Dave,

What are you de[...]?

Enjoy the read.

Ric

To DAVE my
adoring FAN!
Keeper Lit!
Dame Commander
Julia GALVIN
Serene ORDER of
LEONARD.

The Puffin Diaries

Spontaneous travel to the strangest of places

with Rich Shapiro

Illustrations by Christo Roos

**Grosvenor House
Publishing Limited**

Cover design by Nic Grobler
Illustrations by Christo Roos

This book is published by
Grosvenor House Publishing Ltd
Link House
140 The Broadway, Tolworth, Surrey, KT6 7HT.

Proceeds from the sale of 'The Puffin Diaries'
will be donated to Birdlife International, to support their work
in the conservation of puffins and other seabirds around the world.

www.facebook.com/puffindiaries
By email: puffindiaries@gmail.com

A CIP record for this book is available from the British Library

ISBN 978-1-78623-362-2
E-BOOK 978-1-78623-363-9

For my amazing wife, Jacky, and our girls.

What a wonderful world...

To the many strangers who travelled

with me awhile, and became my friends

Contents

CHAPTER ONE

Providence

Over the Greenland Sea
May 22nd — 65°34'23.46"N, 37°08'03.69"W

'Have you seen this view? Isn't it wonderful?' I asked the man next to me on the plane, irritated at his indifference to the spectacle of icebergs, mountains and cloud outside my window.

It was a Saturday afternoon, and sitting aboard a twin-engined Fokker 50, inbound to Kulusuk on the east coast of Greenland, at the wrong time of year and with no pre-arrangements in place, it crossed my mind that this might be an appropriate way to begin three months of spontaneous travel across the world.

Far away Greenland has been on my bucket list for a long time, so it became the first destination of what I hope will be an interesting few months in the northern hemisphere. I've travelled from South Africa, via London, and a connecting flight from Iceland.

I tried to make enquiries about accommodation in Kulusuk, but my internet search revealed little, and the few photos promised a barren, pretty sort of place with lots of water. My emails to the Kulusuk Trading Post went unanswered for weeks, and so I gave up, trusting in providence.

Providence provided me with a window seat on the right-hand side of the plane, and a gentleman passenger on my left, whom I studiously ignored, as is my habit on aeroplanes. In a small daypack under my seat were three black leather-bound Moleskine notebooks, which I hope to fill with travel stories in the coming weeks and months.

Bad weather obscured the prospect of a view as we headed across the Danish Straits. I adjusted my iPod to find the most appropriate accompanying music and settled on Irish anthems, in a collection titled *Long Journey Home*. Given the swirling clouds and the shaking of the plane, it all seemed rather appropriate!

Gradually the clouds began to thin, affording glimpses of a deep blue sea, capped with many 'white horses'. After several minutes of staring, with a sudden jolt to the heart, I realised that these were not white horses, but pieces of ice, drifting on the waves.

I performed contortions on my seat as I snapped dozens of photographs and began to be irritated by my neighbour's complete disinterest in the view. The clouds intervened again, and for the next few minutes I tried vainly to analyse strange shapes thrust upwards at me through the tapestry of white.

I turned away from the window to change the settings on my camera, and when I looked again, it was all there. In the distance, a spectacular range of snow-drenched mountains covering the horizon and beneath them, a white carpet of cloud stretching out towards me. Below, gaps in the cloud revealed great shelves of ice, separated by dark water.

It was a real moment in time for me, and I battled to take it all in, my face pressed against the glass. The man next to me remained unmoved. I gazed in wonder at the ice shelves for several minutes, trying to absorb the grandeur of it all. Eventually, I could bear it no longer and turned to him and asked, 'Have you seen this view? Isn't it wonderful?'

'Many times,' he replied, 'I live in Kulusuk.'

'I'm Johann Brandsson,' he said to me, smiling, introducing himself.

'Johann Brandsson from the Kulusuk Trading Post?' I asked, seeing confusion on his face, and not ready to believe in such coincidence.

He nodded at me strangely.

'I've been emailing you for the past few weeks, trying to find accommodation.'

Amazingly, incredibly, having given up on email and internet, and trusting in providence and 'the god of whims and prayers', my own personal tour guide was sitting right beside me as we descended through the light cloud and made our final approach low over a magnificent bay filled with icebergs and islands.

As the wheels touched down and we landed in Greenland, my reverence for providence and all things unplanned was unbounded.

Next to the runway, on a bed of fresh snow, stood the Eskimos and their dogs.

CHAPTER TWO

Please Sir, But Where Are You From?

In the mountains near Kulusuk, East Greenland
May 22nd — 65°34'43.70"N, 37°09'03.17"W

I followed the tracks of the dogs and their sledge as I trudged my way through the snow, occasionally sinking below my knees. Soon they left me far behind, and I was on my own, in a valley of snow, with mountains all around.

My euphoria at the chance delivery of my personal tour guide and the surprise Eskimo welcome was gone, torn away from me by a few worrying revelations from Johann, all in the form of questions:

'Did you not bring any food?'

'Why are you here out of season?'

'Where are your skis?' and

'Are you sure you're warm enough?'

Just a few minutes later, I was alone in the snow – Johann and his family had disappeared on their snowmobile, and the Eskimos and their dog sledge were racing away with my backpack. The other passengers from the plane all left on helicopters to Tasiilaq, wherever that is.

As it was out of season, the road between the Kulusuk airport and village was snowed in, and we had to trek out of the valley on foot. Well, I had to, it seemed!

'At least I have the valley all to myself', I wondered, looking nervously around for polar bears. On the wall at the airport, I'd seen the skin of a polar bear, and was told it had been shot last year on the runway, together with its mate.

Johann had pointed vaguely at a ridge between two mountains and suggested that if I could get to there, I would see the village in the valley below. 'Thankfully there is no danger of darkness overtaking me,' I thought, as the sun was still high in the sky.

When I'd boarded the plane from Reykjavik this morning, I had noticed how many people were wearing North Face jackets and pants. Here in the northern hemisphere, the north face of a mountain is the one that is always in the shade, making it the colder side. I had been proud of my First Ascent jacket but stuck there in the snow, I imagined a deeper symbolism!

I trudged on, surrounded by snow and self-doubt.

The news headline, *Explorer accountant, aged 38, eaten by polar bear on first day of three-month sabbatical,* flashed before my eyes. I've set out to see new places and meet interesting people on this trip, but I want to be able to 'follow my nose' and not be restricted by plans. I do realise this goes very much against my training and profession! Alone in that valley of Greenland snow, instead of three months of random adventure, I envisaged a posthumous Darwin Award for stupid death.

As I neared the ridge, I found myself in a small graveyard filled with large white crosses. There were perhaps twenty graves, each with a wooden cross and entirely covered in bright plastic flowers – the pinks, purples, reds and yellows providing a vivid contrast to the landscape of white around me.

I walked on, and as I reached the ridge and looked down into the valley beyond, I was forced to stop for several minutes to take it all in.

I could see in the distance a jagged peninsula of snow-covered mountains, and a frozen sea beginning to yield to spring at its edges. Below me, overlooking the melting waters of the bay, I could make out a collection of brightly painted wooden houses and could hear the distant sound of huskies calling.

Later, I found myself alone in a small house used by backpackers in the summer months and the prospect of no food until the trading store opened on Monday morning, some thirty-six hours away. On entering the house, I found the floors covered in dead insects and had to sweep them out into the snow. The temperature hovered around zero and although the sun was out; it didn't make too much difference.

'There is,' Johann had told me when apologetically showing me my lodging, 'a small hotel in the next valley which may have some food. It'll be a bit of a hike through the snow.'

After spending a little time in my sleeping bag weighing up my options, I opted for the one that would get me away from the dead bug house and closer to the food. I emptied my backpack of clothes and, wearing most of them, headed off into the snow once again.

4

A long time later and out of breath from my exertions, I found myself at a blue, two-storey hotel overlooking a narrow frozen sea and mountains beyond.

The hotel foyer was deserted. Standing there, with a small puddle forming around my feet, I called out 'Hellooo, is anyone here?' a few times, my voice echoing in the empty foyer. There was no answer.

I wandered into the downstairs lounge and the office, calling all the time. Eventually, I heard a noise at the top of the stairs, and a short, thin man with brown skin came bustling down, straightening his shirt. He appeared surprised to see me.

'The chef has no food,' he said to me when I asked. 'There are no guests at the hotel.'

My mind worked overtime. 'Could I have a drink at the bar?' I countered, and he relented. 'Of course, of course.'

On entering the upstairs bar, I immediately noticed the adjoining dining-room and a table beautifully laid out for ten people and covered in food – a mouth-watering starter, baskets of bread and bottles of wine.

The little brown man stepped between me and the food. 'That is a private function, sir – the airport staff have arranged a dinner in preparation for the season, sir,' he said, looking at me uncertainly.

'The chef has no OTHER food, I'm afraid, sir,' he added, correcting his earlier statement.

Ordering a beer, I sat beside the window, and looked out for polar bears on the frozen sea, all the while thinking to myself – 'Must find an angle here, must find an angle.'

The beer arrived, a Tuborg Danish Pilsner, along with the chef himself, who had come to apologise. He was a big man, Scandinavian in appearance, with white hair and beard, a rather large stomach and dressed, as chefs do, all in white. At Christmas, he would make for a rather convincing Santa Claus!

'I am very sorry sir,' he said, bowing a little and looking away from the wet patches on my knees, 'but we ordered in the food especially for the function.'

He nodded at me vigorously, egging me on to accept defeat.

'You have no other food in the kitchen – not even a sandwich?' I asked. He hesitated, and I could smell triumph.

'Let me see what I can do,' he winked and bustled off to his kitchen.

I had enough time to finish my beer and scan the horizon for wildlife before he reappeared and approached my table, beaming.

'One of the guests is unable to make it this evening, and so we have one portion extra,' he announced.

'Would that be acceptable, sir?' he asked as if there might be any doubt. He didn't know my other options were beer and dead bugs.

The menu went something like this:
Fresh bread rolls with Danish butter
Starter: Two fillets of cold Norwegian salmon, served on a bed of shrimps and dressed with salmon roe and cucumber
Main: Slices of beef fillet served with new potatoes, whole roasted garlic and courgettes and covered with a rich cheese and mystery sauce
Dessert: Baked strawberry muffin-sort-of-cheesecake-thing, dressed with peaches and icing sugar

As I ate, they turned on some light background music, but quickly changed this to Elvis Presley's *Hound Dog*. I enjoyed my dinner looking out over a polar landscape with a most unexpected accompanying soundtrack. The bread rolls and the Danish butter went into my jacket pocket as backup for breakfast.

At the end of the evening, the chef approached me once again and asked, 'Please sir, but where are you from?'

'Oh, I'm from South Africa,' I answered. He looked confused for a moment and then gestured out into the snow.

'No sir, where are you from?'

I pointed to over the mountain and said, 'Oh, just from the village,' and he nodded his head very slowly and backed away, his eyes betraying his wonderment.

I wiped my mouth with a dainty napkin, layered myself with clothing and headed out into the night.

CHAPTER THREE

The House Where I Live

Kulusuk Village, East Greenland
May 23rd — 65°34'04.82"N, 37°11'13.71"W

This morning I awoke in my bug- and food-free wooden house on the hillside, to the sound of huskies calling. I pulled up the blind and looked out over an arctic landscape beginning to stir for the summer. The mountains all around were still covered in snow, but the frozen lake outside my window had begun to thaw. A steady stream flowing beneath a wooden pedestrian bridge cut a deep channel in the ice as it wound its way towards the sea. Just beyond the lake, an overhang of snow clung to the top of the cliff, waiting to fall.

Kulusuk Village has about fifty wooden houses, randomly scattered across a rocky hillside, and nearly all occupied by Inuit families. The word 'Inuit' means 'the people' and they were formerly referred to as 'Eskimos', which means 'eaters of meat'. Nowadays they prefer to be called 'Greenlanders'. In the summer months, Kulusuk is an island, separated from the Ammassalik peninsula by a narrow stretch of sea. For most of the year though, it is frozen over, and they are joined.

Many of the houses have their own set of huskies outside, strategically tied up so that they can't reach each other and fight. A few of the friendlier ones are allowed to be together it seems. The huskies stay outside, rain or shine, summer or winter, but it is winter that they come into their own, with the dog sledge the primary means of transport.

My house is actually the backpackers' hostel and has three rooms – a downstairs kitchen and living room and a large upstairs sleeping loft. There is a small toilet, but no bath or shower. In fact, I don't think there is running water anywhere in the village, and everyone seems to fetch their water from a central point. My house sleeps ten people comfortably, but as the only idiot here out of season, and with the dead bugs gone, I have it all to myself.

In the living room there is a metal drum that looks a hundred years old and burns crude oil or whale blubber or something, and keeps the house remarkably warm if you know how to use it. After a long time trying to light it, I swallowed my pride and went for help. Johann came to my rescue but when he lit it there was a whoosh of flame, and the drum shook terribly for a long time. In my efforts to light it I had apparently fed it with enough oil to warm an Inuit family for a month!

We fled to the next room and made small talk about our lives until the danger had passed. I told Johann about my career in a big four accounting firm and how taking a few months off for extended travel had worked so well for me in the past, giving me fresh insights and energy for the next phase of my career. He spoke about how he and his family split their time between Denmark and Greenland, and about the highlights that a Greenland summer can bring. He also asked about my family, and I spoke about my dad who'd passed away just two years before, and about my mom and four elder sisters. He was interested to hear about my girlfriend, Jacky, and how we'd cope being apart for three months. 'She is hoping to get leave from work and join me for the last few weeks,' I said, which seemed to pacify him!

Johann spoke about his training as an anthropologist and his interest in the Inuit people, who are hunters and fishermen, spending their days hunting seals, or the occasional polar bear, and fishing. There are very few jobs for the local people, and their options are limited. Apart from the hunting and fishing, and some ivory and bone carvings for tourists, they have little else they can do. The government pays for all education, up to any level, and any person not formally employed gets a weekly welfare grant. The foodstuffs and other items in the Kulusuk Trading Store are heavily subsidised by the government.

Although it has its own government, Greenland remains strongly linked politically and economically with Denmark. Ninety percent of the population of Greenland are Inuits, or Greenlanders, and the balance, mainly Danes.

When the metal drum eventually stopped shaking, Johann said his goodbyes and I sat down to my bread roll and Danish butter breakfast. As that only took a moment, I was soon outside, wandering the village and hiking out into the mountains, gaping and gawking at the beautiful scenery. There were no trees and the only vegetation was a motley collection of brown grasses and spongy moss. In the summer though, according to Johann, it is a rolling mass of green.

9

Near my house, I found the carcass of a seal that looked as if it had been there a long time, altered in shape now and then by someone hacking off a chunk to feed to their husky, or the occasional gnawing by a husky pup on the loose. Because of the cold, there was no smell, either from the carcass or the husky turds littering the snow.

This afternoon I noticed several people lying on the frozen lake, fishing through a hole in the ice. As I neared them, the ice gave way beneath me, and my one foot slipped through into the frigid water below. The fishermen quickly came to my aid and guided me to where they were fishing.

'Hvad laver du her?' a young Inuit man with a fur-lined poncho asked me, nodding vigorously.

Realising that he meant 'What the hell are you doing walking about on the thin ice?' I changed the subject and pointed to his friend, face down in a hole in the ice.

'You fish?' I asked, stupidly, nodding.

Ponchoman and I quickly came to understand each other, and he showed me their catch of about ten small fish that looked similar to mullets. I pointed at my empty stomach and showed Poncho a banknote, and he agreed to sell me some food.

After a few minutes, I enlisted Poncho's help in getting me safely off the ice and retreated to the warmth of my little house, my oil stove, a can of baked beans and sausages that Poncho had provided, and myself for company and conversation.

CHAPTER FOUR

One Person Short Again

On the dog sledge, East Greenland
May 24th — 65°34'43.70"N, 37°09'03.17"W

'You must be the guy they are talking about up at the hotel,' she said to me, smiling and shaking my hand. 'I'm Raggi.'

'You must be the guy they are talking about up at the hotel,' she said to me, smiling and shaking my hand. 'I'm Raggi.'

Raggi had long, light-brown hair and wore a bright red ski jacket and a happy smile, and was very interested in solving the mystery of the hotel's guest from the snow.

This morning, after being the first customer of the week at the Kulusuk Trading Store and stocking up on food, I started exploring in earnest. Walking down to the still frozen harbour, I noticed three or four dog sledges coming at high speed across the snow, laden with passengers. I quickly made my way down to where they had stopped and happily photographed the beautiful husky dogs getting all tangled up in their ropes. It was a tour group of Taiwanese people who had arrived on some circuitous route from the hotel. Their leader was Raggi. She made a bee-line for me and got straight to the point.

'Yes, that's me – the mystery guest who ate all the food,' I laughed, 'my name is Rich.'

After suggesting to her tour group that they wander around Kulusuk for half an hour, she began to quiz me on what I was doing here and to answer my similar questions about herself.

Raggi is in her late twenties and grew up on the fjords of western Norway. She has only recently arrived in Kulusuk having been employed by the hotel as their full-time guide. At age nineteen she moved to England, and, among other jobs, for the past five years she has been the postlady in a remote hamlet of western Scotland, called the Isle of Rum. One of twenty-five applicants for this job in Kulusuk, she said it was her ability to live happily in remote places that got her the position.

Raggi and I have one thing in common – we both know very little about Greenland. For my part that's okay – I'm a tourist. For her part it's a problem – she's a tour guide! She has been told that if she does not know the answer to a question, she should make something up!

One of her tour group came up to her while we were chatting, and asked where the school was. Raggi just smiled and pointed confidently up the next hill. When the lady had begun the climb, Raggi looked at me and said, 'It is up there, isn't it?'

Raggi introduced me to the driver of one of the dog sledges and I was given a personal introduction to the world of huskies. I was fascinated how each dog was attached to the sledge by a rope of differing length, and how this was done in a particular order, based on the personality and behaviour of the dog.

'To stop them fighting,' chipped in Raggi, 'they tie up one of their front paws near their neck.'

As this new information had come from Raggi, I wasn't sure if she'd just made it up, so I did take a closer look at the dogs, and spotted a few with a paw tied near their neck.

'If you like,' Raggi said to me as they were about to leave, 'you can come back with us on the dog sledge. We're one person short.'

A flood of déjà vu washed over me!

Before she could change her mind, I grabbed my chance and found myself at the front of the sledge, with a Taiwanese couple behind me, hanging on to me for dear life. The man seemed to have his work shoes on, and had covered them in plastic packets so they wouldn't get wet! I'd finally found someone more under-dressed for Greenland than me.

Behind us, standing on the back of the sledge and manning the brake and the whip, stood the Inuit guide extolling his dogs with sharp yips and cries. After being tied up, the dogs seemed to relish their freedom and charged out into the fray when they got their chance, the wooden sledge bouncing off the occasional rock along the way. The dogs are huskies, but that is a generic term for similar breeds. More correctly, they are known as Greenland dogs and are incredibly adapted to the cold. They live outside, and in the cold, they stick their head into their stomach, curl up into a ball, and wait out the weather. They survive thanks to a unique double layer of fur that insulates and protects against the extreme cold.

Sitting there on the dog sledge, with the Taiwanese man's arms around my waist and his plastic packet shoes on either side of me, I felt my mouth break into an involuntary grin as the huskies charged ahead and the cool Greenland air swept up against my face.

When we reached the hotel, and the tourists were sent on their way, Raggi gave me a grand tour, in a welcome so different to just a few days ago. I joined her and a few colleagues in the bar and for an hour or so we drank Danish beer and spoke about the world as if we weren't really in a faraway place shrouded in ice. I got to meet a few of the staff who had sat down to their fancy meal the other night, while the stranger from the snow shared their fare in the other room, listening to *Hound Dog*. I was keen to hear more about huskies and polar bears, but most of the talk was about Denmark and Sweden's chances in the upcoming European football championships.

Before too long the Taiwanese started drifting in, needing attention, and my friends dispersed to their various duties. I headed for my wooden house on the hillside, courtesy of a snowmobile driven by one of my new Greenland friends.

CHAPTER FIVE

The Killing Fields

In the drift ice, East Greenland
May 25th — 65°32'05.67"N, 37°13'14.29"W

Pele (pronounced Pi-leh) is a very important man in his village. He must be because he has the biggest boat. Pele, however, like his country-men, is not big. Standing perhaps five foot two inches tall, and with remarkably short, stubby legs, he is broad of shoulder and has a wide face that breaks easily into a smile. He has lost at least three of his smiling teeth.

The harbour of the village of Kulusuk or, more accurately, the place where about a dozen small boats are lying, is wherever the ice ends and the sea begins. The men of Kulusuk drive their boats up onto the ice as if it were a sandbank, clamber off and walk home. No anchors, no ropes, no need. There are no waves here, no great tidal movements.

Pele's big boat is about twenty feet long and has a cabin and a large black Mercury engine. It also has a green awning that encloses the whole boat in inclement weather, which they have a lot of here. Many of the boats do not even have cabins.

When the weather is clear in Kulusuk, and sometimes when it is not, the men hunt. It was an early afternoon start, and Johann arranged for me to accompany Pele on his hunt for seals. I had that wary, butterfly-in-the-tummy feeling as I picked my way across the ice, wondering about such things as single engines at sea, ice-bergs, sudden squalls from the east, the killing of seals and so on!

Pele, on the other hand, had none of these concerns and gave me a big, broken-tooth smile of welcome.

'You are welcome,' he said, showing me where to stand to help him push the boat off the ice. I would soon find out that Pele's English vocabulary was limited to only about ten words, restricting the afternoon to gestures and the nodding of heads.

Nearby, two hunters were settling into their boat and drinking out of a suspicious looking brown bottle. I assumed it was for warmth, although perhaps it was for luck or courage. When the bottle was empty,

14

they casually tossed it onto the ice, where I assume it will remain until summer, and then sink.

Apart from Antarctica, Greenland is the least populated place on the planet. Dominated by mountains, it is one massive wilderness area, with only a few human settlements, and eighty percent of the land lies under a permanent sheet of ice, at times up to three kilometres thick. It has fewer than sixty thousand people, most of whom live in the southwest in towns like Nuuk, Narsarsuaq and Kangerlussuaq. Here on the east coast, Kulusuk and Tasiilaq are the only settlements for hundreds of kilometres.

Bundled up in beanie and jacket, long johns and gloves, it was a sublime feeling speeding out across the dark waters of the channel, gazing in awe at the mountains all around and heading out into the distance where icebergs and a long wall of drift ice awaited us.

Once we had cleared the channel, we followed the coastline to the north, up around the back of Kulusuk Island. We passed beneath the overhangs of big icebergs that were fifty or sixty metres high in places, some so large that they sustained their own little stream of water cascading off into the ocean below. They were walls of solid ice, enormous blocks of white, punctuated here and there by a fault line of deep blue running diagonally across the ice.

Seabirds wheeled and cried as we passed, and I squinted to make out the weird and extraordinary shapes that the icebergs made as they emerged out of the haze – one a cathedral spire, one an enormous man sleeping on his back and another the Sydney Opera House.

We found ourselves in a channel between two vast floes of drift ice, one up against the land and the second out in the ocean. The channel itself was about a kilometre wide and perhaps a few kilometres long, with several groups of icebergs floating in strange formations within.

But we were looking for seals, searching for the distinctive black head or rolling back of the ringed seal, either on the surface of the water or, if we were 'lucky', on the drift ice itself. Pele's eyes scanned the waters like a metronome, and now and then he raised his binoculars to his eyes. Then, just as we neared a horseshoe section of the landward drift ice, he squealed excitedly and pointed into the distance. I saw nothing but ice and water.

He gunned the engine, and we raced forward and around to where he had seen it. I think he was trying to drive the seal towards the ice.

Then I saw it, the small black head on the surface, twisting 180 degrees, looking, looking. Pele slowed down, driving right around the seal and edging up towards the drift ice where, to my great surprise, he rammed the boat up onto the ice and leapt off, gesturing wildly at me to pass him his rifle, telescopic lens mounted on top. He also grabbed a long wooden pole with a metal spike at the end and hurried off across the ice to a place where he could hide behind a big mound of snow.

For a moment I thought he was singing to himself before I realised that he was calling to the seal. Hiding behind the mound of snow, he laid the rifle to one side and began making high-pitched squeals and at the same time scraping the metal spike along the ice, creating a rasping sound that I assume makes a seal curious. For a long time there was no sign of the seal, and just when Pele seemed ready to give up, I saw it, only fifty metres from us, head out of the water, twisting from side to side, listening, listening. I could see its big dark eyes and its whiskers.

It was no contest. Pele grabbed his rifle, resting it on the snow mound, and with a boom that I think is still travelling across some distant ice floe on the Arctic Circle, fired a bullet through its brain.

A certain numbness settled on the upper half of my body as I helped Pele push the boat back off the ice and we raced to retrieve the body. A pool of blood hung just beneath the surface, and, some metres away, bits of yellow brain lay on the water.

The seal had sunk.

'Sunket,' said Pele, crestfallen.

'Sunket,' I repeated, the bile in my throat.

The Inuit people are hunters, as they have been for many centuries. There is no agriculture – everything revolves around hunting, and the seal is their prime target. The Greenland government, recognising both the cultural history and the fact that there is nothing else to do here, pays the hunters for seal and polar bear skins, actually at above the current market rate. That is their job.

We continued in silence, following the edge of the drift ice, Pele looking out to sea for seals, me scanning the drift ice in the hope of not seeing a polar bear. Polar bears are often seen here, and the Kulusuk hunters kill several each year. Fortunately, no non-Inuit persons are allowed to shoot polar bears, so hunting safaris are out of the question.

However, if we saw one, Pele would try and kill it, and I definitely didn't want to be around for that!

After passing several beautiful icebergs, Pele heard on the radio about a sighting, and we raced off towards a distant iceberg, glistening in the late afternoon sun. As we rounded the berg, we found ourselves in a small bay with the drift ice on the landward side and two groups of icebergs guarding each end. A veritable killing field.

Three Inuit boats were already in the bay, searching. The search did not last long. Close by, not fifty metres from our boat, popped up the heads of two enormous hooded seals, eyes bulging. Bobbing there in the water, they looked almost friendly, curious, intrigued as to what these boats were doing here. The one even looked at the other, its long whiskers dragging on the surface.

The boat nearest the drift ice was quickest to react and its skipper, like a Native American Indian on horseback, stood over his steering wheel and aimed his rifle at the dark heads, from barely thirty metres off.

Two shots rang out and a third from a boat more distant. Pele did not fire. I was sure the seals were dead but, inexplicably, the shots had missed, and the shooter swung his boat round in a frustrated circle and watched for the heads to reappear. They did, briefly on the other side of us, looking back at us, as if to say, 'What the hell was that?'

Then, before the hunters could fire, they dived and despite a half hour search by the boats, were not seen again.

As we returned empty-handed to Kulusuk harbour, the early evening colour painted in the sky, I imagined a different outcome to our day – the boat filled with dead seals and even a polar bear, the blood spilling at our feet, and my spirit haunted by demons for all time.

CHAPTER SIX

When the Isle of Rum comes to Greenland

Atop Mount Rich, Kulusuk Island
May 26th — 65°33'39.10"N, 37°05'09.78"W

Off the west coast of Scotland, there are about eighty islands close to the mainland, which are referred to as the Inner Hebrides. Just below The Isle of Skye, which is the northernmost and largest of these islands, lie the Isles of Rum, Eigg, Muck and Canna. The Isle of Rum is inhabited by only thirty people and is custodian to a herd of that most unusual of breeds, the Highland cow – long, shaggy-haired cattle that look continually depressed. They are cared for by Stuart, a Scotsman with a long, shaggy ponytail of hair hanging down his back. He also looks after a herd of Highland ponies and keeps an eye on the golden eagles, and the red deer as well. It's a big responsibility.

Ragnhild Rostrup (or Raggi) was until most recently the postlady on the Isle of Rum, which paid the annual salary of five thousand pounds. That seems a lot of money for being postlady to only thirty people. Raggi, on the other hand, thinks differently.

'You have to sort the mail first,' she said with a deadpan face, 'then you have to deliver it.'

'And then,' she sighed deeply, drawing out the story for my benefit, 'you have to collect NEW mail, and sort it AGAIN, and send it off!'

She looked at me, with big eyes for extra emphasis.

'It's quite a job, you know!'

Stuart, sitting beside her, nodded slowly in agreement.

'Aye,' he said, 'it's a big job.'

After five years as postlady to Highland cows, Raggi felt it was time for a change and is now newly installed as the tour guide at the Hotel Kulusuk. Stuart, her former boyfriend from the Isle of Rum and 'keeper of the cows', is visiting her here, albeit for just a few days.

I can imagine the sudden confusion on the Isle of Rum, with the shaggy cows and ponies wandering the island, looking for their mail.

In my search for people who speak English, I have befriended Raggi and Stuart, and it has been fun hearing stories from each other's lives.

Raggi does not know much about Greenland and answers most of my questions with a deep-throated Norwegian chuckle, a little lean forward in confidence and a whispered, 'I have no idea – don't you know?'

She also has a vivid imagination and enjoys making up stories for future use on her Taiwanese and American tourists.

This evening she commandeered the hotel's 4x4 vehicle and drove Stuart and me up the eight kilometre road to the US Army Radar Mast on top of the island. Halfway up we came across a derelict stone building, and I wondered aloud, 'What could that have been?'

'Oh, the old stone quarry,' piped up Stuart, to great chortles of laughter from Raggi. 'Of course,' she said, 'the old stone quarry.'

'What could they have needed the stone for, I wonder?' she said mischievously, eyeing me in the rear-view mirror.

'The building of the dam, of course,' I said authoritatively, and Stuart added, 'Yes, the dam, the ill-fated dam...'

'Washed away in the great flood of '94,' added Raggi and we all roared with laughter.

Our view from near the top of the island was magnificent – the distant snow-covered mountains of the Ammassalik peninsula, the sheer cliffs all around, the pack ice hugging the land straight beneath us and the spires of icebergs poking through the great cushion of fog that hung like a cloth beneath us.

In a moment of madness, at nine o'clock at night, in the bitter cold and with fog sweeping in off the sea, we thought it might be nice to climb the nearby mountain and reach the highest point, where we could get a 360-degree outlook. A good while later, huffing and puffing, we had summited and gazed in wonder at the extraordinary views.

'What is this mountain called?' I asked Raggi, quite innocently, and very out of breath. 'Why, Mount Rich, of course,' she said, laughing at the world, 'or at least that's what I'll call it if they ask!'

We descended safely and sat together on a bank of snow, throwing pebbles in the river – a Norwegian, a Scot and a South African – chilling out in the coolest place on earth.

CHAPTER SEVEN

Farewell to Groenaland

Kulusuk Village, East Greenland
May 28th — 65°34'04.82"N, 37°11'13.71"W

In the late tenth century, Thorvald Asvaldsson, banished from Norway for murder, took his family and followers to Iceland. A generation later, his son, who came to be known as Eirikur Raude, or Erik the Red, killed two men and, like his father before him, was banished. They fled west again and discovered the world's largest island, which has over forty thousand kilometres of coastline. Erik named it Groenaland in the hope that it would attract people because it had a beautiful name.

Apart from a brief period in the summer months, if you're in the right part of Greenland, it is not green of course. In fact, when they made a television series of the story of Sir Ernest Shackleton and his ill-fated trip to the South Pole, they filmed it right here, so comparable is the scenery to the Antarctic.

In the time that I have been here, there has been a complete transformation in the scenery. The sun has shone, the snow has melted rapidly, and dirt roads have begun to appear as if by magic. A grader cleared the road between Kulusuk village and airport, and I walked it today, looking up at the three-metre high snow banks on each side, and recalling my lonely journey on foot from the airport.

The same road becomes the main road through Kulusuk village, a brown, sand and gravel road that today had rivers of melting snow running down the hill. At the bottom, a little Inuit girl wearing gumboots and bright red trousers played in a puddle with her equally red toy wheelbarrow. She smiled happily at me as I walked past and climbed the hill to the Kulusuk Trading Store.

Friday is the busiest day of the week for the Kulusuk Trading Store, as I found out today on my final visit there. The locals queued up at the little post office to collect their weekly welfare grant and then, inevitably, headed next door to the trading store to spend it. It created something akin to a carnival atmosphere as most of the locals emptied out of their homes and gathered in the shop and its surrounds.

20

The store is a veritable general dealer, and a visit there takes one back to the movies of old – the westerns and their little 'provisions' stores. This provisions store, however, had all the bells and whistles and really was a one-stop shop. From foodstuffs to cookware, from toys to stationery, from what looked like seal jerky to tobacco, from booze to movies, from clothing to fishing rods, from fast food to high-powered rifles – this little store had it all.

I saw many of the people I'd met this week in and outside the store, including Pele and Poncho. I met their families and saw how they were clothed in western clothing with the occasional exception being sealskin boots or fur-lined hoods, perhaps from the arctic fox.

The children ran happily all over the village, smiling and laughing, and many of them had bicycles and the toys of any western child. The one bad habit they learned from their elders is that of littering, with empty bottles and general litter lying between the boulders, in the roads, and in the snow.

I leave today for Iceland, to keep a rendezvous with an Australian friend of mine with whom I share a passion for amateur zoology. We enjoy going to strange places, and seeing the local wildlife, without the help of tour guides. I've said my goodbyes to Johann, Pele and Poncho, and also to Raggi and Stuart. Stuart's parting words were, 'Come visit me in Rum sometime.'

Last night, I sat in my little kitchen, trying to write something akin to the grandeur and spectacle of this place. It was a fine evening with wisps of fog sweeping across the melting ice on the lake, and the call of the huskies was again in my ears.

Behind me, out the back window of my house, a small ridge was covered in boulders, with a husky standing on the largest one silhouetted against the setting sun. Now and then he stood and stretched out his front legs, straight and taut. He pointed his chin toward the heavens, closed his eyes and from a primeval place deep within, came the ancestral howl of the husky, a ROOOOOOOOO that reached a crescendo in a little shriek. Soon the entire village was enveloped in a cacophony of sound as the huskies of Kulusuk answered in unison.

Sometimes, when one is hugely frustrated, driven to the brink, one might let out a groan, or perhaps a shriek, some sort of noise that comes from deep inside. Conversely too, when one is triumphant – utterly, euphorically happy – one might scream out in triumph, not just a Yay, or Yahoo, or Hurrah, but something louder, longer – a string of vowels that cascade out, releasing one's joy.

This place has that sort of feeling, something deeper is required.

Behind me, on the ridge, my husky stood and stretched, a silhouette against the setting sun.

He pointed his chin to the heavens and began to howl again. When he finished, for a moment there was silence, and I went and stood at the open window, bidding goodbye to this strange and wonderful land.

He points his chin to the heavens, and begins (51)
When he finishes,
to howl. for a moment there is silence, and
I stand there in the open window, bidding
goodbye to this strange and wonderful land.

KULUSUK   ICELAND

'The House Where I Live'
Me, Myself and My Husky

'The Killing Fields'
The boats of Kulusuk harbour

'The Killing Fields'
Pele, the hunter, draws the seal nearer

'When the Isle of Rum comes to Greenland'
Raggi and Stuart

'When the Isle of Rum comes to Greenland'
The view from the top of 'Mt. Rich'

'Farewell to Groenaland'
The view from my back window

CHAPTER EIGHT

The Great Icelandic Puffin Hunt

The Cliffs of Vik, Southern Iceland
May 31st — 63°24'26.74"N, 19°01'34.75"W

First, let me make the necessary introductions:

1) The puffin, that most extraordinary of Icelandic birds, stands about twenty centimetres tall. It is a chubby little bird, dressed in black and white, with a bright orange beak that is disproportionately large for its size. It is a distant relation of the penguin, which only live in the southern hemisphere, while puffins are only found in the north.

2) Grant Robinson, or Robbo, my Aussie friend from a long time ago, has flown from London to join me here in Iceland and participate in our self-styled Great Icelandic Puffin Hunt. Some people may say that he looks a bit like a puffin, but I think that is harsh and uncalled for.

3) Sigga, our B&B owner here in Reykjavik, fits very squarely into the typical B&B owner mould – friendly, very friendly, exceptionally friendly, inquisitive and overflowing with helpful advice. Sigga is the trip coordinator, route advisor and puffin specialist on the Great Icelandic Puffin Hunt. Thankfully, hers is only a desk job.

Robbo and I share a history of these sort of trips - where we go to an unusual place and set off on a quest to find the local wildlife, on our own. Our greatest adventure was in Tasmania, an island off the south-eastern coast of Australia, where we searched in vain for the extinct Tasmanian Tiger. Aided by a small rental car and some alcohol, we did find wallabies and wombats, quolls and kangaroos, echidnas and Tasmanian Devils.

Now that the preliminaries are out of the way, let us move on.

Iceland has approximately ten million puffins that nest here during the summer months. Primarily nesting on the many islands that are dotted around Iceland, some of the more intrepid birds also find nesting spots on the mainland, according to Sigga, who knows a lot about puffins.

Tourists who come to Iceland naturally want to see the puffins. And the tour operators of Iceland have realised this and have come up with a myriad of ways for tourists to see puffins. All of these involve going to the islands as part of a boatload of other tourists and gawking at thousands of puffins too scared to nest on the mainland.

Robbo and I decided that, on this trip, we'd definitely like to see a puffin, but not in the usual touristy way. We wanted to find those intrepid puffins who were brave enough to nest on the mainland. The thought of being stuck in a boat with a bunch of tourists and being shown a puffin did not sit well with us. In fact, at Sigga's B&B we'd had enough of other tourists already. Part of a Serbian ice-hockey team was staying in the room adjoining ours and, as well as having no interest in puffins, also made a lot of noise.

A more problematic guest of Sigga's, in the sense of puffin watching, was a noisy American who used the letter 'J' as part of his name he introduced himself by. He insisted on greeting everybody in the breakfast room collectively with a 'Good morning Y' all'. I have also overheard him asking Sigga, 'Do you take AMERICAN DOLLLAARS?'

Robbo and I were a little frightened that J. Whatsisname might be on a puffin cruise boat with us, together with his delightful wife, Tammy or Amanda or something. So we took Sigga into our confidence.

'We'd like to find the puffins, on our own,' whispered Robbo, peering around the room for eavesdroppers.

'On the mainland,' I added, 'we have a car.'

'No problem,' said Sigga, 'I can show you exactly where to go. You'll definitely find puffins.'

Day One of the Great Icelandic Puffin Hunt:
Armed with a plethora of maps, bird books and guidebooks about Iceland in general, all courtesy of Sigga, the trip coordinator for the Great Icelandic Puffin Hunt, we headed south from Reykjavik and into the southwest corner of Iceland, known as the Reykjanes Peninsula.

Nothing could have prepared us for the lava-strewn landscape that lay before us, occasionally clad in bits of moss – a deserted wasteland across which even the cold winds of the North Atlantic hurried quickly to reach more attractive climes. There were no birds of any description, let alone puffins, to lift our daunted spirits.

Sigga's directions led us to the Great Lighthouse of Valahnúkur, where seagulls wheeled in fright at our arrival and fled to the cliffs of Valabjargagja. We took this as a sign and followed. Carefully we climbed the paths leading to the cliffs and inched on our stomachs to look over the edge. There were thousands of birds nesting on the cramped and narrow ledges. Thousands of birds, but no puffins.

'Bloody puffins,' said Robbo.

Tired and dispirited, we searched the coastline all the way to Grindavik and returned home to Sigga in the late afternoon, empty-handed.

'Did I say west of Grindavik?' asked Sigga, looking confused. 'No, that's not right, you must go east of Grindavik,' she said, marking two points on the map. 'Those are the cliffs – you WILL see them.'

Day One of our Great Icelandic Puffin Hunt ended over a few Jack Daniels (me) and Johnnie Walkers (Robbo) at the B&B and a friendly greeting from our American friends, just back from their puffin cruise to the islands.

Day Two of the Great Icelandic Puffin Hunt:

Our spirits sagged as we headed back into another empty corner of Iceland, and spent many hours navigating rocky and ill-kept dirt roads in our tiny aqua-blue rental car. Coincidentally, we were even dressed for puffin hunting, in mostly black clothing and bright orange jackets. I also had a white beanie that I'd bought in Greenland.

After interrupting an Icelandic scout camp to ask directions, and fighting the continued boredom of lava fields, we came to the cliffs at Selatagar, a barren, windswept stretch of coastline, haunted by the cries of the gulls and perhaps a long lost fisherman or two. We parked the car and walked all over the coastline, discovering the ruins of an ancient Viking or Norse fishing village, some interesting driftwood and devising new swear words to aim at Sigga, our tour planner.

A little despondent, we even joked about puffins being a fabled creature that no one ever saw. 'There're no bloody puffins in Iceland,' muttered Robbo. 'Never have been!'

Back at the B&B, we quizzed Sigga when she had actually seen these puffins. 'Oh, four or five years ago, I think. I'm sure they were puffins,' she said. Robbo held me back, and he changed the subject to dinner. Sigga was unfazed.

'I can recommend a restaurant that serves puffin,' she said and proceeded to tell us how puffins are not protected, and are caught by 'sky fishing', which basically means using a very large net to catch a flying puffin. The 'catcher' dresses in orange to attract the puffins!

The fresh heart of a puffin is apparently an Icelandic delicacy. I know I'm keen on unique experiences on this trip, but eating the heart of the same bird that we're searching so hard to find really didn't seem right.

Day Three of the Great Icelandic Puffin Hunt:

'There're ten million puffins in Iceland,' said Robbo at breakfast. 'We can't find one.'

Sigga was her usual bubbly self.

'I have a plan,' she said.

'Why don't you go on the boat from Reykjavik harbour? In one hour you'll see ten thousand puffins.'

We both glared at her.

'Then you'll have to go to Vik,' said Sigga.

Our two and a half hour drive southeast from Reykjavik led us through a panorama of sheer cliffs, waterfalls and glaciers. For once the lava landscape had given way to green farmlands, filled with Icelandic sheep and the beautiful Icelandic horses with their hairy manes.

Buoyed up by our drive, we arrived in the tiny seaside village of Vik, situated alongside towering cliffs that dropped straight into the ocean. There were no puffins immediately in view, but our spirits were greatly lifted by the sight of a roadside hotel, Hotel Lundi, which had, as its logo, a large puffin dressed in top hat and tails and holding a walking stick. In case the guests didn't know what it was, at the bottom of the logo was the word *Puffin*.

We literally danced through the door, expecting puffins everywhere.

The reception was deserted. Robbo led the way into the dining room and found an Icelandic girl laying tables. She had short cropped black hair and wore a light brown zip-up jumper. She seemed surprised to see us, and her hands fiddled continuously with the zipper of her jumper.

'We're looking for the puffins,' Robbo said. 'Can you tell us where to find them?'

She looked at us as if we were mad.

'I'm sorry. I'm new here. I don't know anything about puffins.'

Zippergirl obviously hadn't seen the sign outside!

At the entrance to the dining room, right next to me, there was a stuffed puffin, at eye level in a hole in the wall. I nudged Robbo.

'This is a puffin,' said Robbo pointing, sounding like he'd actually seen one before.

'You could try next door,' she said, letting go of her zipper for a moment and pointing towards the nearby gas station.

The friendly clerk at the gas station was much more helpful and enthusiastically asked several other shoppers about puffins. They all agreed that there used to be lots of puffins a few years ago. As for now, they had no idea.

We left, dejected.

'Maybe they were hunted to extinction.' said Robbo. 'Bloody puffins.'

As a final throw of the dice, we visited the local souvenir shop, where we hit the jackpot when Robbo befriended a pretty girl with big boobs, wearing a low cut tank top.

'Puffins, you say? Well, they're all at sea during the day you know, feeding. But come nine o'clock at night – you'll find them way up in the cliffs over there,' she said, pointing to the dark foreboding cliffs.

'Well, it's lunchtime now,' I said to Robbo. 'We can't wait here till tonight.'

'Let's go climb some cliffs,' said Robbo, smiling.

I wasn't sure if Robbo wanted to spend more time with the pretty girl or ask her to point some more, but he led her to the book section and picked out a wildlife book, and showed her some puffin pictures.

'I just wanted to make sure she really knew what a puffin was,' he lied.

We drove our car as far as we could and then set off on foot to the end of the walking path. No puffins. Lots of seagulls, but no puffins.

We began to climb around the base of the cliffs, skirting bright green vegetation that was thickly inhabited by seagulls. They jealously guarded their nests as we carefully climbed past them.

'Rich,' called Robbo, quietly, pointing into the distance.

'A puffin,' he whispered.

There, on the edge of a grassy overhang, midst the gulls and the spray from the waves, stood a puffin, alone against the world, staring fixedly out to sea.

It was a feeling of achievement one cannot easily replicate, a sense of discovery. No cruise ship led us here, no tour guide – we found it ourselves – our very own puffin.

Excitedly, like Livingstone at the Victoria Falls, or Darwin at the Galapagos, we clambered our way further up the cliffs and manoeuvred onto a ledge directly above our little puffin. It was unperturbed and allowed us to photograph it to our hearts' content.

Soon there were others, all around us, diving in the wind or just sitting quietly nearby, waiting to be photographed.

The Atlantic puffin is an amazing bird. In the coldest months of the year, they spend six to eight months bobbing about in the North Atlantic, far from land, their bright colouring turning drab and grey. They mate for life, and each spring they return to the same place to nest, with bright orange bills and feet. They raise one chick, who looks like a puff-ball, which is where the puffin's name originates. Puffin chicks are called pufflings. Atlantic puffins can dive up to sixty metres below the sea to find their food which is usually sand eels and small fish. They can carry up to fifty fish in their bill at one time.

But the most important thing about puffins is that, if you look hard enough, if you really deserve it, you will find them.

Robbo and I clung to those cliffs of Vik, at the bottom of Iceland, for a very long time this afternoon, entranced and enchanted as the puffins of Iceland found their own special way to end our Great Icelandic Puffin Hunt.

Robbs and I clung to those cliffs of Vik,
at the bottom of Iceland, for a very long
time this afternoon, entranced and enchanted
as the puffins of Iceland found their own
special way to end our Great Icelandic
Puffin Hunt.

CHAPTER NINE

Professor Puffin

Reykjavik, Iceland
June 1st — 64°17'14.60"N, 21°05'01.09"W

Having spent the better part of three days being misled and misdirected by the Icelandic locals, Robbo and I took some pleasure in our hard-won status as puffin experts.

It started almost immediately when we returned from the cliffs of Vik and found a tourist standing near our rental car, taking in the scenery. Even though he didn't appear to be about to climb the cliffs of Vik, Robbo was undeterred. 'Do you know where to find the puffins?' he asked, and before the man could answer, proudly gave out very specific instructions on where to find them.

We laughed afterwards, and it quickly became a mission to re-educate those who had wronged us. Robbo's 'girlfriend' at the souvenir shop was genuinely pleased that her directions had helped, but our main target was the lady at the Hotel Lundi. With me secretly recording on video, Robbo led the way into the hotel and found Zippergirl, this time behind the front desk. Robbo pretended that our earlier visit never even happened, which confused Zippergirl even more.

'Excuse me,' he said, 'could you tell us where we could find puffins?'

Her hand went straight back to the zipper, and she stammered in complete confusion. She reached up to get some brochures, and Robbo decided enough was enough.

'Hang on,' he said, 'we can tell you where the puffins are,' and he did.

Of course, our greatest enjoyment should have come in returning triumphantly to Sigga's B&B, and regaling the story of our day, Jack Daniels and Johnnie Walkers in hand. However, the guests of the previous day had departed, and Sigga just said, 'Didn't I tell you that you should go to Vik?'

This morning at breakfast, still pleased with our success with the puffins, and unsure what else to do, we asked Sigga for suggestions.

'You can't come to Iceland and not see the Gullfoss waterfalls and The Blue Lagoon,' she said, and so it was decided.

First stop were the waterfalls which were spectacular, but apart from a stray duck, were without any animal life to speak of. We also visited the historic site of Pingvellir, which was the site of the first government of Iceland. There we learned more about the story of Erik the Red, who had discovered Greenland, but only after he had been expelled from Iceland for murder. As it was at Pingvellir that the first parliament was set up in 930 AD, it is likely that the first laws were also established here, and perhaps Erik the Red had been banished at this very spot.

After Erik and his followers had spent three years exploring southern and eastern Greenland they returned to Iceland and told fabulous and fanciful stories of the green, green land they had discovered. Erik the Red found however that his enemies had not forgotten him, and he decided to start afresh in Greenland. His stories of the land of green tempted nearly five hundred Icelanders to join him, although many were lost on the voyage to Greenland. Erik the Red had a son, Leif Eriksson who, around 1000 AD, ventured further west and became the first European to set foot in North America. To understand Leif's name, Icelandic names have an original first name plus the suffix *sson* or *dottir* after the father's first name.

Erik the Red is the central character in framing for me the story of Greenland and Iceland, two lands whose names should probably be exchanged. That legacy is thanks to a wild man with long red hair, a bad temper and the spirit of adventure in his bones.

After a light lunch of a dozen puffin hearts (I'm joking), we headed to 'The Blue Lagoon', a series of turquoise geothermal pools about fifty kilometres from Reykjavik, and Iceland's premier tourist attraction. However, we quickly bored with lying about in pools, which were 38 degrees Celsius and lined with white mud (silica). After some debate as to what to do, we agreed that we were definitely the most knowledgeable puffin experts in the whole of Blue Lagoon, and we should make the most of it. We covered our heads in white mud and had fun approaching unsuspecting tourists and talking to them about puffins. Stuck there in the mud with us, so to speak, they were a captive audience. Their usual reaction was to smile and try and converse, but their eyes looked wildly around of their own accord and gave them away. Robbo's main line of questioning to the wild-eyed tourists was about the lifespan of a puffin, and the consensus seemed to be about six or seven years. Robbo, who should perhaps be renamed Professor Puffin for his persistence, enjoyed giving them the correct answer of twenty-five!

Professor Puffin and I are now heading to London, where I'll be for the next few days as I work out my next place of most opportunity.

Perhaps Erik the Red, on his Viking ship, had the same philosophy!

'The Great Icelandic Puffin Hunt'
Rich and Robbo, high above the town of Vik, and below, the very first puffin

CHAPTER TEN

The Virgin Sailor

Ouistreham Yacht Harbour, Normandy
June 4th — 49°16'25.61"N, 0°14'54.13"W

'You'll just have to lie,' said Robbo, frying eggs on his stove, wearing just his work trousers and a black and white striped apron. Robbo's wife, Becs, hovered nearby, making coffee.

'You know how to do that, Richie, don't you?' she laughed.

We were in their West Hampstead flat in London, and I think they were trying to make sure I ate properly, at the same time as being envious of my current freedom to travel in any direction at a moment's notice. Overnight, I'd had a phone call from a friend who I'd briefed to be on the lookout for unusual travel opportunities, and he'd found one. There was a flotilla of yachts leaving Portsmouth imminently for France, to commemorate the D-Day landings, and an Admiral he knew was looking for crew for his yacht.

'You do know how to sail?' my friend had asked me.

'Of course,' I'd replied, and then spent the night worrying about the implications. I knew nothing about sailing, and hadn't been on a yacht since a junior school sailing trip that hadn't stayed afloat.

'I've already lied,' I said to Becs, buttering my toast and eyeing out the bacon and mushrooms that Robbo was lining up for me. 'I'm sure that lying about it will get me on the boat; the problem is that I have zero sailing skills to back up the lie,' I said, filling my plate with food.

'Yes' said Robbo, 'but getting onto the boat is the most important part, and in any case, if it works out badly, the story you write will be even more entertaining.'

'Very funny,' I said, sitting down at the kitchen table.

'I bet you're wishing Jacky was with you now,' piped up Becs, passing me my coffee.

Becs is a big fan of my girlfriend and constantly on my case about me taking the 'next step'! She also knows that Jacky is a very good sailor, having grown up with boats.

'Oh well,' I said, 'I guess I have no choice. Portsmouth here I come!'

Later that day my large backpack and I arrived in Portsmouth and I found my way to the small boat harbour, feeling very self-conscious amidst all the people with practical hats and canvas shoes.

The 'Admiral' I was to meet was actually a retired Lieutenant-Commander from the Royal Navy, but if I was to pretend to be a sailor, then I think he could be called an Admiral. I'd been told that he'd been a submarine commander for much of his life, and I was even more daunted when the directions I'd been given led me into the shadow of an enormous submarine that I later discovered was HMS Alliance, a naval submarine museum. A little further along I came upon the yacht I was looking for, named *Jemmana*, but there was no one in sight. I could see that the door to the cabin below had been opened, so I called out 'Ahoy' and 'Hello', but only the seagulls replied.

Leaving my backpack near the yacht I retraced my steps toward the carpark, and soon came across an older man with a ponytail and blue overalls. 'Are you the Admiral?' I asked.

He stopped and looked at me as if I was mad. 'You must be f***ing joking, mate?' he said, and walked off.

Pulling myself together, I made it to the carpark, where I found an athletic, silver-haired man wearing shorts and a light blue short-sleeved shirt, offloading boxes from the back of a car, with the help of a woman and a younger man.

'Are you John Phillips?' I asked, a lot more confidently, and when he smiled at me, I said, 'I don't know anything about sailing, but I can lift heavy things.'

My admission of guilt broke the ice, and I was quickly introduced to his wife, Jo, and the other 'sailor', Lyndon, who was shirtless and 'blister-red' from too much sun. I helped carry the provisions to the yacht, and after a brief tour, was given all the menial tasks that required no seamanship whatsoever.

Nearly twenty four hours later, I was standing at the helm of Jemmana, its sails catching the wind above me, as I steered her towards the French coast, looming ever closer through the light fog. It was hard not to think back to June 6, 1944, and the thoughts of the Allied soldiers on seeing the same view.

I experienced my own panic when the Admiral said to me, 'Why don't you take us in, Rich?'

With very light winds, the Channel crossing had taken twice as long as usual, which had provided me the opportunity to learn about the world of sailing, from the very best. After passing my 'basic' training in the first part of the voyage, I was even entrusted, in the wee small hours of the morning, with watching out for the navigational lights of the big ships. Perhaps most enjoyable though, was the camaraderie below deck, and sitting with my new friends around a small table on the high seas sharing spaghetti bolognaise and funny stories.

Steering Jemmana towards France, I managed to find the channel leading to Ouistreham, a small town on the Normandy coast, just a few kilometres from Caen. As we approached the harbour, a Brittany ferry that took up most of the channel, decided to leave port and I turned to the Admiral and said, 'I think this is where you come in!'

He did, and we managed to evade the ferry, before mooring in a lovely yacht basin filled with perhaps a hundred boats, all flying their most festive colours, and calling out greetings to old shipmates found at last.

Later, as we sat down to dinner in the Admiral's cabin, with beautiful wood panelling all around and the company of new friends, I shook my head at my hesitations about sailing and gave thanks for new skills learned.

A sailor at last. Well, sort of.

  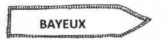

OUISTREHAM   BAYEUX

CHAPTER ELEVEN

Bicycling Bobby

Bayeux, Normandy, France
June 5th — 49°16'10.41"N, 0°41'51.76"W

I found her at the bus station, that meeting point of the paths of weary travellers. Bus stations, not airports, sometimes train stations – a hub where down-to-earth, interesting people sit around idly or run around confused, where their overloaded bags tear at their shoulders, and their faces tell stories; a place where the waiting passengers make eye contact with each other, and conversations begin.

I had come from Ouistreham, on the forty-minute bus to Caen, capital of Normandy province and the connection point for my bus to Bayeux. My destinations were the villages of St. Laurent and Vierville, and Omaha Beach, the slaughterhouse of D-Day all those years ago.

Just off the bus from Ouistreham, I found myself at the back of a long queue for an information desk that was manned by a sweaty Frenchman. As is customary for me, I had no idea what time my bus to Bayeux would leave and resigned myself to the process of queuing. An elderly lady and her bicycle, however, did not. It was difficult not to notice someone trying to push a bicycle into a bus queue!

She stood about five foot four and looked about eighty. She wore a big, green anorak and dark brown walking shoes. She was slender and had long whitish hair that looked like it might once have been blonde. She had tried to tie it up into a bun, but clearly, the bicycle riding had wreaked havoc with her hair for it stuck out of the bun in all directions. She looked a little crazy. After all, she was trying to push a bicycle laden with bags into the front of the queue.

Because of her height, the sweaty Frenchman didn't notice her at first, but the chap at the front of the queue certainly did when the bicycle wheel pushed between his legs. From the back of the line, I could not hear what was said, but it ended with the sweaty Frenchman pointing out into the car park where a bus was closing its doors. The old lady rushed her bicycle out of the bus station, bags swinging dangerously from both sides of her handlebars.

'Silly old bat', I thought to myself.

Then a most remarkable thing happened – the silly old bat pushed her lopsided bicycle in front of the bus, forcing it to stop and leaving the bus driver, a big man with a bald head, gesturing wildly with his arms.

He opened the doors to shout at her, and she tried to push the bicycle up into the bus. When no one else seemed interested in helping her, I abandoned my place in the line and ran to the bus. The silly old bat was peering up into the bus, the front wheel of her bike on the bottom step. She couldn't understand what he was saying.

'But this is my bus,' I heard her say, in beautiful English, her accent very British, her voice quite soft. She was in a complete tizz.

'Let me help you get on the bus,' I said and took her bicycle from her, looking up at the bus driver with eyebrows raised.

'OK, OK,' he said, gesturing with his hands at her to get on.

'This is the bus for Bayeux?' she asked him again, and I realised this was the bus I needed. Providence was being kind to me again.

'Bayeux, oui,' said baldie bus driver, nodding.

'I must fold up my bicycle,' said the lady, her cheeks soft and sagging with age.

'Fold up the bicycle?' I looked at her as if she was mad.

Then she produced an empty canvas bag and started folding her bicycle, the bus's passengers now craning their necks to watch. It really was a fold-up bicycle! Once a hinge in the middle was unclipped, the two wheels swung on top of the other and clipped together, and the handlebar twisted down alongside them. I seemed to be helping rather than hindering, but just as we finished she looked up at me with a blank haze in her grey-blue eyes, and said,

'What are you doing? No, let me do it,' and promptly began to reassemble the bike.

I averted the eye of the bus driver.

She came to her senses. 'Oh, no,' she said, 'why am I putting it together? We must take it apart. Here, can you help me?'

She pushed the bike toward me, and I undid it again and fitted it neatly into the canvas bag while she nattered on to the bus driver about something. She didn't seem to care that she was delaying the bus.

'Oh,' she said, pushing a sleeping bag at me, 'this needs to go in there as well.'

'Sleeping bag?' I thought. 'What on earth is this old girl doing in the middle of France with a sleeping bag and a fold-up bicycle?'

I squashed the sleeping bag in with the bike, zipped up the bag and carried it up into the bus. There wasn't time to put it into the hold. She clambered quite nimbly into the bus and sat near two British army guys who were talking loudly about pubs and sore heads. I sat on the other side of the aisle, but close enough to join in the conversation.

She chatted happily with the Brits, all about the pubs in England and they compared notes about the channel crossing the night before.

'Slept on the floor I did,' she said proudly.

'Those damn seats don't go back far enough.'

She cocked her head to one side, recalling her night on the ferry. When one of the Brits moaned about his sore head and regretted spending so much time in the pub, she quickly retorted, 'Oh, don't say that – pubs are great.'

She hails from Leamington Spa in Warwickshire and is here in Normandy for the anniversary of D-Day. She comes every ten years or so, she said, mainly for the big anniversaries, and has some friends in Bayeux with whom she hopes to stay.

'I did write them a letter a few months ago,' she said to us, 'but haven't heard from them – hope it's ok.' Her voice trailed off.

'Oh well, I've got my sleeping bag if they don't have room. I'll just go to the camping ground – that's where I stayed last time.'

We were all leaning in closer to her now, her soft voice and fascinating story drawing us in. I wanted to hear more. 'How old was she? Did she have family?'

'I'm hoping to find Danny the Red,' she continued, her eyes dancing. 'I saw him at a pub here last time – first time in fifty years – he put me up at the house he rented.'

'Why's he called Danny the Red?' one of us asked the obvious question. It turned out that she knew Danny before the war and he used to have lovely red hair.

Somehow the conversation turned to the Iraq war.

'Idiots. Bloody Iraqi War. I was in the protest march in London, you know, before they went to war,' she said, talking directly to the two Brits. 'And I was in the House of Commons when they approved it.'

45

She threw her wrinkled hands up in the air.

'Couldn't believe it! Still can't.'

She lapsed into silence as the bus drove through the streets of Bayeux. The silence didn't last long.

'Now that's a nice pub,' she said, rising in her seat and pointing.

The bus pulled into the station, and I carried the bike down into the street and began assembling it.

'Who are you?' she said, peering at me blankly, her mind deserting her for a moment. I looked back at her, amazed, but she seemed to come to her senses.

'Oh, you helped me board on the other side, thank you again.'

I introduced myself properly, hoping to get her name.

'Bobby,' she said firmly. 'With a 'y' of course.'

'Waters', it said on her luggage tag. Bobby Waters.

The two British army guys helped me tie her bags to her bike, one bag on the rear carrier and two further bags, one hanging from each handlebar, at her insistence. It looked very dangerous.

'Oh no,' she said to one of them, 'I don't ride it. God no, I push it!'

The two Brits said their goodbyes, and she called after them, 'Hope to see you down at the pub tonight!' They smiled at each other. She wasn't kidding!

'Could I take a photo of you with your bike?' I asked, and added, 'For my mum.'

After she had posed, I said, 'You're an amazing woman. Could I ask how old you are?'

'Eighty effing five,' she said, clicking her tongue crossly. 'It used to be great to say I was in my seventies, but not eighties,' she said, shaking her head, her hair tumbling about.

'Anyway, better be going,' she said brightly and trundled off.

I watched her disappear down the little hill, pushing her bike, parcels waving from side to side. Just near the town square, under a canvas of fresh green poplar trees, she turned the corner and was gone.

I watched her disappear down the little hill,
pushing her bike, parcels wavering from side to side.
Just near the town square, under a canvas of
fresh green poplar trees, she turned the corner and
was gone.

FRANCE

LONDON

'The Virgin Sailor'
Getting ready to cross the English Channel

'Bicycling Bobby'
Bobby Waters in Bayeux, Normandy

CHAPTER TWELVE

A Message from my Haggis

Fort William, Scotland
June 14th — 56°49'01.45"N, 5°06'44.39"W

A maxim I am increasingly relying on in deciding where to travel to rent is 'Put yourself in The Place of Most Potential.

A maxim I am increasingly relying on in deciding where to travel is 'putting myself in the place of most potential'. Where will I find people most interesting, the culture so different, the wildlife so unusual, the challenge most daunting?

It's a maxim by which to live one's life.

Having returned after a few extra days in France visiting the Normandy beaches, my dilemma was whether to spend a week staying with Robbo and Becs in London and watching the European soccer championships from the couch or the pub, or going elsewhere. Tempted as I was to stay home and relax, that's not what this was all about. It wasn't the place of most potential.

That is why I found myself in McTavish's Kitchen in the western highlands of Scotland, in a town called Fort William. The highest mountain in Britain, Ben Nevis, was nearby and the deep waters of Loch Linnhe lay alongside. The town is also where the West Highland Way, a famous walking trail, finishes.

I am en route to the Isle of Rum, to take Stuart up on his casual invitation to 'come visit me in Rum sometime'. Not sure he expected me almost immediately! It's involved an EasyJet plane flight to Glasgow and a three-hour bus trip along the edges of Loch Lomond, a famous elongated finger lake synonymous with whisky, fishing and golf. As one might expect of Scotland, it was raining during the bus ride, and the

50

mist hung heavily over the lake and in the trees, providing me with a soulful introduction to the highlands of Scotland.

I tried to find something Scottish on my iPod for accompaniment and ended up listening to Billy Connolly jokes while watching the rain fall.

The menu item that caught my attention at McTavish's Kitchen was the following:

HAGGIS & NEEPS – Haggis served with bashed neeps and champit tatties

I ordered it. The dish of most potential.

Fort William, although the largest town for miles around, remains small and tranquil. The highest mountain, the deepest loch and loads of history – it turned out to be the ideal place to spend an evening. In one corner of the little restaurant, an authentic Scottish group were setting up, dressed in kilts with tartan jackets.

Tomorrow morning I'll catch a train to a place called Arisaig where I hope to find a boat that will take me to my place of most potential, the Isle of Rum.

My haggis and neeps arrived, together with a curious look from my waitress.

'What's haggis made out of?' I asked, looking suspiciously at the brown lump on my plate.

'Oh, bits and bobs, you know,' she said carelessly, avoiding eye contact and skipping away quickly.

I leaned forward, investigating with my nose. There were three good-sized lumps on my plate, of equal size. The white lump I identified as the champit tatties (potato), and I assumed the orange lump was the bashed neeps (turnips). That left the brown lump as the haggis.

It smelled a bit strange, but ok, just a faint whiff of something I couldn't quite put my finger on...

I took a big swig of my ale, and worked my fork into the brown mush, giving myself a generous helping. I remembered my late brother-in-law, Alan, saying how important it was to address your haggis before eating.

I addressed my forkful of haggis. I said, 'Haggis, be nice,' and I ate.

It had a creamy taste, soft and a little crunchy. It was somewhat nutty, with a hint of the unusual.

'Definitely meat in here somewhere,' I muttered to myself, taking a swig of ale before eating some more.

'A bit too dark for normal meat though', I thought, but I was hungry, and pushed on through and cleared the plate.

When I was done, I called the manager over, and asked, 'Could you tell me how you make your haggis?'

'Umm,' he said, looking at me uncertainly, then changed his mind about something and said to me, 'It's mashed up mutton, sir,' and walked off, leaving me exploring between my teeth with my tongue, in search of answers.

My main course, homemade steak pie, arrived and the Scottish band got under way – one bloke on accordion, another on a fiddle, a young guy called Euan on the bagpipes, a schoolgirl called Maeri doing the Highland dancing and an older woman singing lots of favourites. They started with a good old Scottish waltz and moved on to other favourites like *The Devil in the Kitchen*, *The Highland Fling*, *Roamin in the Gloamin*, *My Bonnie lies over the Ocean* (*my granny went down to the cellar*), some poems from Robbie Burrrrns and, of course, *Scotland the Brave*.

After my afternoon drive along Loch Lomond, and my inner tussle with the place of most potential (which road to take this week), my favourite song was *The Bonnie Banks o' Loch Lomond*, and whether to take the high road or the low road.

The singing and the last of my pint cleared my mind and my palate of the mystery of the haggis, although a strange flavour remained. The manager reappeared at my table.

'Now that you've finished your meal, sir,' he said to me mischievously, 'I thought I'd tell you more about the haggis.'

I looked at him blankly, my tongue on the move again. 'I wasn't entirely truthful about the minced mutton, sir,' he said, speaking softly, leaning in towards me.

'It is from the sheep, but it uses all the bits that nobody else wants, if you know what I mean, sir?' he said, winking at me.

'I hope you enjoyed it,' he said.

'Oh yes,' I said, in a deep Mr Bean voice.

A few more minutes of the bagpipes and the fiddle, and I could feel the first signs of indigestion – a series of soft, quiet, repeating belches – bringing with them each time a little message from my haggis.

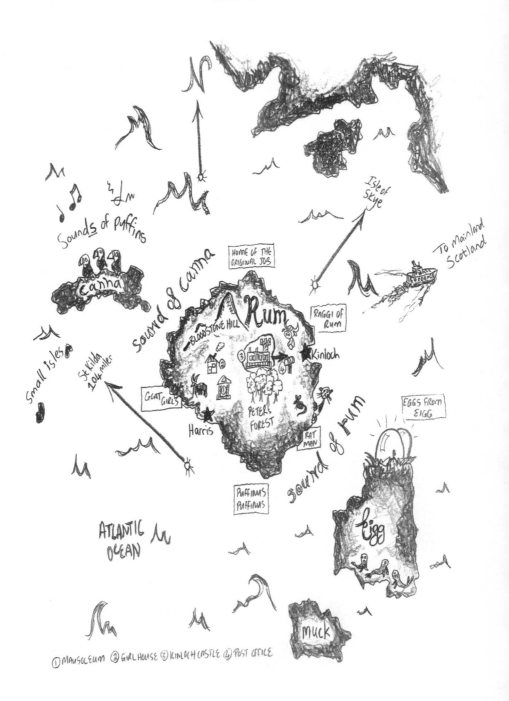

CHAPTER THIRTEEN

Balls to the Wall

The Isle of Rum, Western Scotland
June 15th — 57°00'56.89"N, 6°16'51.52"W

It is a scene of devastation, a murder scene. The old stone courtyard is still and quiet, but there's blood on the floor today. Hamish and Harry lie prostrate on the cold stone, dead to the world, the blood still dripping from their wounds. I pick up my camera and zoom in on Harry's head. In the frame, just above his ears, his two balls, swollen and bloody, stare back at me, angry and alone.

It was a scene of devastation, like a murder scene. The old stone courtyard was still and quiet, but there was blood on the floor today. Hamish and Harry lay prostrate on the cold stone, dead to the world, the blood still dripping from their wounds. I picked up my camera and zoomed in on Harry's head. In the frame, just above his ears, his two balls, swollen and bloody, stared back at me, angry and alone.

Twenty minutes earlier I had held Hamish and Harry's heads and stroked their beautiful manes. They were Rum ponies, a breed of Highland pony, that famous Scottish breed. Their coats were shiny and well cared for. Their manes were shaggy and long. They were friendly and lovable and trusting.

What had we done?

One hour earlier, I had arrived on the Isle of Rum, off the west coast of Scotland, by ferry from Arisaig. Also on the boat was a dead ringer for James Herriot, the fictional travelling veterinarian – a big man, casually dressed and carrying his toolbox of terror.

Standing on the quayside, dressed in his blue working overalls and wellingtons, was Stuart.

'Greetings Rich,' he'd called and come forward to shake my hand. 'Afternoon, Chris,' he'd greeted James Herriot and helped me lug my backpack off the boat.

There was no settling in, no leisurely tour, no coffee and catch-up. 'Let's cut off some balls then,' said Chris, causing me to frown rather quickly.

There aren't many big events in Rum, an island of only thirty people and a few tourists. In fact, even the most mundane, the smallest event, is a big event. Chris, or James Herriot to me, comes to the island about four times a year and each time it's a big event. By the time we'd reached the stables, a small crowd had gathered around Hamish and Harry, stroking them gently, talking to them sadly. Hamish was tan coloured with a beautiful blonde mane, and Harry was grey.

They had reached the age at which, if their testosterone was not somehow reduced, they would gradually become unmanageable, and not be of much use as working ponies.

'They've already started misbehaving,' Stuart had said on the short drive from the ferry.

James Herriot is a very good vet. Balding in the middle of his head, with long grey hair on the sides, he had that air of quiet confidence about him, and his practical clothes and easy sidestepping of pony dung added to the image. He established firm control from the start.

'Let's all be calm, everyone, no unnecessary noise,' he said, in his best bedside manner, as he and Stuart gently held Hamish's head. Hamish's blonde mane seemed to mingle for a moment with Stuart's long brown ponytail as they stood there, side by side. Stroking Hamish's head softly, the vet quietly slid the needle up into the vein on Hamish's throat, and two minutes later, Hamish was down on the stone, a rope pulley attached to his hind leg, and the scalpel poised in his crotch.

'He's sure got a big pair on him,' James Herriot said softly, holding them in his left hand. With a quick incision along the side and a bright spurt of blood, he squeezed the offending testicle from its pouch and slashed and cut a few ropes and pulleys that trailed after it. He tossed them casually away, sewed up the cut and repeated the procedure on the other testicle.

After a few sprays of secret mixtures into Hamish's nether region, he stood up and said, 'Right you go, Harry, your turn now...'

The crowd and I seemed to take an involuntary step backwards as Harry was led forward. When it was over James Herriot marched smartly past us, his hands covered in blood, and the small crowd followed, hoping to catch his ear about their dog, or their cat, or perhaps themselves. I stayed, watching over my ponies and began taking a few photographs.

There was a tap on my shoulder.

'Oi,' said Stuart, handing me a long stick, 'this is a working holiday,' he laughed. 'We need you to help us with the cows.'

Leaving my camera and bag beside the horses and their discarded bits, I followed Stuart and a few others to a nearby paddock where a herd of enormous cattle awaited us. These were not ordinary cattle. These were the famous Highland cattle – great shaggy beasts, their long hair and curling horns giving them the look of the woolly mammoth.

'Watch out for their pointy bits,' said Stuart, circling the herd and scaring them back towards me.

The cows were much larger than normal cows and their shaggy coats and long spreading horns that point forwards and sideways gave them a fierce look. My stick looked powerless in comparison. I waved it aimlessly towards them, like a twig at a rock. 'Mush,' I said.

It seemed to work and they veered off and I survived. In between the herd were the young calves, looking like giant teddy bears. Today was the day for the teddy bears to have their big snip.

'Don't worry about their fierce looks,' called Stuart, as a large, black cow swung towards me, 'they're quite docile. Watch out for...'

'Their pointy bits,' I finished his sentence for him, 'Yes, I've noticed.'

We brought the herd up to the stables where James Herriot took command once again, and the gathering took on a rodeo feel as the teddy bears were separated from the mothers and placed in a small enclosure, ready for the cutting. Stuart and Sean, another 'keeper of the cows', were to be instructed on how to de-ball a teddy bear.

It was an amazing scene: One of the keepers pinning the calf against a grating, another holding its tail in the air and Stuart kneeling in the mud, gripping its testicles and injecting anaesthetic into them. James Herriot crouched on top of Stuart, bloody scalpel alternating between his right hand and his mouth, his chosen place of storage. All around was the hubbub of the fascinated crowd, interspersed with frantic

Highland moms, bellowing their moos into the mountains above. The discarded testicles were tossed casually into the nearby woodpile, trailing their strings behind them. Danu the Labrador dug them out and devoured them, his eyes gleaming.

When it was over, James Herriot was quite the picture with blood smears on either side of his mouth from the scalpel, a few spots on his head and his hairy arms caked in red. Danu the Labrador attracted some attention for a while when the anaesthetic in the testicles had the same effect on his tongue, and it lolled about uncontrollably.

The blood and gore lulled the crowd into silence. Ed, the Rum Reserve Manager, said loudly, 'Aw, come on guys, finish up now! In my day, we'd be drinking beer already and frying up the balls in butter.'

Much later, a few of us sat around an old wooden table outside the Isle of Rum General Store, drinking beer in the evening sun. As Danu had eaten all the balls, we had to make do with peanuts and crisps. James Herriot had been and gone, his duties completed. He'd done the ponies, he'd done the calves, he'd checked out a few dogs, and he'd swapped a few stories. The locals were disappointed he didn't stay over, as he often does.

'Perhaps in September,' he'd said, as he waved us goodbye at the ferry.

It is day's end on the Isle of Rum, and while I still feel sorry for Hamish and Harry and the teddies, I'm intoxicated by the adventure of this island and all that it seems to hold. The last light of day catches in the cloud hanging over the island, casting an eerie pall over the nearby castle and deepening my anticipation of tomorrow.

CHAPTER FOURTEEN

The Forbidden Isle

Kinloch Castle, The Isle of Rum
June 16th — 57°00'48.49"N, 6°16'55.20"W

The Isle of Rum. The very name conjures up the image of a dark island, mystical and sinister, swathed in fog and fear, a fortress home for the illegal barons of the sea – peg-legs, parrots and pirates.

Sixty million years ago volcanoes ruled the western half of Scotland, and the isles of Rum, Muck, Eigg and Canna burst out of the sea, their sandstone and granite cliffs jagged and steep. Early Stone Age people populated Rum, and eventually, the Norse and Gaelic peoples of present-day Scotland came to live here – fishermen, bird catchers, farmers and seal hunters. These islands make up what are today known as the Small Isles of Scotland, not far from the Outer Hebrides and the Western Isles. Muck, Eigg and Canna are the closest islands to Rum, and Canna is home to lots of puffins, I have heard.

Arriving on the ferry from Arisaig yesterday, my preconception of Rum was met by the distant scene before me – a dark island, with high mountains and threatening black clouds.

The island is said to resemble the shape of a diamond, its jagged edges formed by the sea cliffs, and its high pyramid centre formed by the Cuillin – the great peaks of Trollaval, Askival and Hallival, the shattered remains of a long-dormant volcano. The island is about sixteen square miles, but there are only two or three small areas where human habitation is possible.

The Isle of Rum takes its name, not from secret deposits of the seaman's friend, but rather from the ancient Gaelic word *Ruiminn* which means 'a ridge of hills'.

As part of the clearances of the 1820's, the inhabitants of Rum were forced to leave the island and were sent to Canada, and the island was then used for sheep farming. In 1886, a wealthy cotton baron from Lancashire, John Bullough, bought the island, and over the next thirty years, his family, and in particular, his son, Sir George Bullough, transformed it into an entertainment complex to show off their wealth to their idle friends. They built Kinloch Castle, a magnificent castle that remains to this day, filled with all the trappings of opulence. George Bullough was knighted by King Edward VII for his services in donating his steam-powered yacht as a hospital ship during the Anglo Boer War.

Wandering through the castle today, I gazed in awe at the reception room with its Steinway piano, its beautiful paintings, the lion, leopard and cheetah skins on the floors, Japanese incense burners, plush curtains and the oversized cloisonné vases, presented to Sir George by the Emperor of Japan. I was further amazed by the beautiful dining room, the fancy billiards and smoking room, the formal lounge, the library, the drawing room, the gallery and the many bedrooms. There is also a strange ballroom, where the windows are high and the servants hatch secret so that no one might peek in. Under the main stairs is an orchestrion, the great musical invention of its age, a forty-piece mechanical orchestra that could be set to play any of a hundred tunes, as guests were arriving or gathering for dinner. It still works. Outside the castle, the opulence continued – Victorian gardens, heated conservatories where nightingales flew, alligator and turtle ponds, redirected rivers, eighty thousand trees and even a hydro-electric plant to provide electricity for the castle. This was Edwardian society at its highest point, a fantastic celebration of wealth and pomp, a venue for the greatest of summer parties.

The First World War changed all that, and of the many staff sent to the trenches, only two returned to Rum. Not considered done to be living such high life after the war, the family seldom visited their castle, and it became a decaying relic of a bygone era. They left everything as it was, even books lying open on the table, waiting to be finished.

Still, the island kept its reputation as 'The Forbidden Isle', and many a stray boat that wandered near its shores had a bullet fired across its bow in warning.

In 1957 the whole island, including the castle, was sold to Scottish Natural Heritage, thereby becoming a national nature reserve. The small sum of £23,000 paid for the island reflected the Bullough family's preference for the nature reserve option. One of their stipulations was that the tradition of providing two deer per year to each household should continue, and does to this day. Stuart is eagerly awaiting his next deer so he can refill his freezer!

Yesterday, on the ferry from Arisaig, we stopped en route at the nearby Isle of Eigg, and I hid my head in shame at the sight of a colony of grey seals, lounging on the rocks. I'm still having flashbacks to Greenland and the outing with Pele. Determined to put that behind me, and encouraged by our enjoyable puffin adventure in Iceland, I set off today to find some local wildlife of my own. I followed the coastline to the south, looking for an otter that was often seen there, or perhaps the white-tailed sea eagles that were reintroduced here in the 1970's. Not only did I not find any otters or eagles, but I was chased back to Kinloch Castle by midges, tiny biting insects that swarm you and deliver very painful bites. I had been told they were the curse of any summer visitor, and I quickly discovered why! As the midges chased me home, it crossed my mind that karma was after me!

The first warden (now called reserve manager) of Rum, who arrived here in 1957, came back for a visit today, and Stuart arranged that he and I accompany Peter Wormell on a reminiscent ramble across the island. Peter pointed in amazement at little forests they had planted and commented on how they'd grown. He showed us canals they'd dug and told us more stories of the Bulloughs' of Rum.

But everything on Rum leads back to the castle - the link between the past and the present. Standing there today, in the great reception room, with stag heads mounted all around and the huge paintings of Sir George and Lady Monica looking down, I could think of more than a few friends of mine who would enjoy the summer here in the castle - a few weeks of idleness, the odd foray into the mountains for a spot of hunting and, in particular, being waited on, hand and foot, with gin and tonics and invitations to dinner.

CHAPTER FIFTEEN

Raggi of Rum

The Isle of Rum, Western Scotland
June 16th — 57°00'55.70"N, 6°16'50.13"W

'Oh, so you know Raggi then?' said the young girl behind the counter of the Isle of Rum General Store, her demeanour changing instantly. She had very long reddish hair that tumbled over her shoulders and onto the counter. The store was tiny and was lined with basic provisions, alcohol and a few handwritten notices. It reminded me of the Kulusuk Trading Store, but on a much smaller scale.

'Aye,' I said, in my new Scottish accent, 'I met her up in Greenland a few weeks ago – she's a bit crazy, old Raggi.'

'Aye, that she is,' said the redhead, her eyes gazing above my head, thinking, 'or so I've heard.'

'My name is Kate,' she said, sticking out her hand. 'I've only been here a few months, so I never met Raggi, but I've heard all about her.'

'That's her there,' she said, pointing to a photograph pinned against the wall. I leaned over, squinting.

'That doesn't look like her,' I said, staring at the photo of a girl with long black hair, a square, dumpy black hat, an ankle length purple skirt and a Mona Lisa smile. 'She looks almost Victorian.'

'Aye, that's her though,' said Kate, 'you'd better ask Stuart – he'll know the story – she was in trouble for something, I think.'

From my very first day on this island, I have realised that Ragnhild Rostrup, or Raggi, casts a very long shadow on the Isle of Rum. In the little General Store, her hand-woven beanies and handbags lie on the shelf, for £8 and £12 respectively, the signs on the wall are in her handwriting, and whenever I ask anyone about her, their eyes light up in delight, and they immediately ask for news and stories of Raggi.

Raggi first came to Rum as a pony gilly, about seven or eight years ago. Pony gillies are responsible for following the deerstalkers in hunting season and loading the carcasses onto ponies. They then lead the ponies back to the village where they help with the butchering and packing of the meat. Not a typical job for a girl, but then Raggi, from the fjords of Norway, is not your typical girl. After a season or two with the ponies in the mountains of Rum, she progressed to become the tour guide at Kinloch Castle, regaling tourists with tall stories of the great Edwardian parties in the castle before the First World War, and supposed sexual escapades with the sailor boys in the ballroom. Perhaps due to these tall stories, or, more likely, due to her forthright manner and loud opinions, she fell out of favour with the Rum Reserve Manager and in particular, his wife.

Stuart told me the story over a dinner of pasta and red deer mince at his little house next to Kinloch Castle this evening.

'She couldn't stand her – Raggi would rub her up the wrong way every time she opened her mouth.'

He took a long swallow of his beer and chuckled.

'They had it in for her; they did,' he said. 'They did a search of her room and found she was using Castle toilet paper, so they fired her – banished her from the island, they did.'

'Banished?' I looked at him in amazement. 'How can they do that?'

'Well, everyone here works for the estate in one way or another – they banished her – she had to go to the mainland.'

Over the next half hour or so, over a few more beers and more than a few chuckles, the story was told.

By that stage, Stuart and Raggi had become a couple, and Raggi was determined to pay a conjugal visit to the island.

'But how?' Stuart had said, 'they'll see you when the ferry stops?'

'I have a plan,' said Raggi, 'I'm coming in disguise.'

They chose a weekend when the Reserve Manager and his wife were going to the mainland, but still had to manage the tricky bit of Raggi getting off the ferry while the manager and his wife got on. Her long black wig, square hat and the Victorian dress did the trick, and they didn't even blink as she walked past them.

As the ferry was casting off from the quay, Raggi, reunited with Stuart and delighted at her success, laughed out loud, one of her distinctive, deep-throated Norwegian chuckles.

Even above the engine of the ferry, her laugh carried to the ears of the departed, and they turned around in horror, too late to do anything. According to a third party on the ferry, who later told the story to Stuart, the manager's wife beat her fists on the side of the boat and remonstrated at her husband all the way to the mainland.

'You're undermining my authority,' Stuart was told by the manager the next week. A short while later, to the great relief of Raggi and Stuart, the manager and his wife left the island and, under new management, Raggi was permitted to return.

This time she got the job of postlady – not a very taxing position, given that there are only thirty people on Rum. I'd had this discussion with Raggi in Greenland, and she'd defended herself to the hilt, listing out the sorting and delivering, the collecting and the re-sorting as quite onerous tasks and, in Stuart's words, 'a big responsibility'.

My subsequent research on Rum revealed that Raggi was indeed the postlady, but that, undisclosed by either Raggi or Stuart, there was also a post office lady, who did all the franking and the 'official stuff'!

This did mean that Raggi had a certain amount of free time on her hands, where she could make a bit of cash on the side. She crocheted the beanies and handbags for the tourists, did occasional gilly work with the ponies, and volunteer work in the Isle of Rum General Store, which despite its small size, also acts as the post office and village pub.

And one winter Raggi became a winkle picker. Now a winkle picker is someone who, obviously, picks winkles. A winkle is something that lives in the sea in a tiny shell, and which the Spanish love to serve as a starter. In the freezing Scottish winters, which unfortunately are the best time for finding winkles, Raggi would be out on the rocks of Rum, dressed in her postal boots and woollen beanie, scrounging for winkles!

All good things come to an end, and Raggi headed off for pastures new, to Iceland and ultimately Greenland, leaving behind a broad trail for me to follow – her footprints deep and clear, her legend intact.

From pony gilly to butcher, from craftswoman to tour guide, from exile to postlady to winkle picker, this girl's done it all.

Hail Raggi of Rum!

CHAPTER SIXTEEN

The Home of the Original Job

Kinloch Village, The Isle of Rum
June 17th — 57°00'54.50"N, 6°16'52.01"W

If you live on the Isle of Rum and you have a normal sounding job, like postlady or castle guide, you are in the minority. For Rum is the home of the original job, the place to come to meet the strangest people doing the weirdest jobs imaginable.

The Rat Man of Trollaval, as he's known here in the village, spends his days on the slopes of Trollaval, Hallival and Askival. These are the three main nesting grounds of the Manx shearwater, a most beautiful and graceful sea bird and related to my friends the puffins. In fact, its scientific name is puffinus puffinus, and Rum has the world's largest population of puffinus puffinuses. Seventy thousand of them breed in the burrowed tunnels where the Rat Man hangs out. I considered climbing the cliffs, but without Robbo to encourage me, I opted for drinking beer in the sun instead, together with Stuart and a few locals.

Strange coincidence, but one of my beer drinking companions turned out to be the Rat Man of Trollaval himself. He explained the mechanics of his job to me while we waved the midges away from our faces, in between swallows of beer.

'I'm investigating the impact of rats on the breeding of the shearwaters,' said the Rat Man, staring at me intently from small eyes, his stubble several days old, and already more impressive than my month-old scraggly beard. I nearly corrected him about the puffinus puffinuses, but he didn't look like he wanted to be spoken to.

'Each day I lay out long wires with sweets at different intervals, on different slopes where the shearwaters breed, and then I analyse the wires to see if the sweets have been chewed on...'

He finished his beer and wandered off, expecting me to surmise the next stage of scientific study. I watched him go, wondering how he coped with the loneliness of all those hours on the mountain.

The job of winkle-picker, after it was abandoned by Raggi for reasons that could range from cold fingers to exile, has now fallen to two burly brothers from Mallaig, who arrive on Rum for several short visits each year, and terrorise the locals. They are fine when they don't have alcohol in them, but are a 'little violent' once they've had a few too many. The General Store at Rum now has a policy of not selling spirits to the brothers Mallaig, limiting them to beer.

The same General Store also sells basic foodstuffs, including:

Eggs from Eigg. Hot from the Bot!

My increasingly good mate, Stuart, the 'keeper of the cows', has one of the more regular jobs on the island, taking care of the Rum ponies and Highland cattle, together with two other 'keepers'. He also ties up the ferry when it makes its daily visit to the island. He lives in a quaint double-storey house just near the castle, together with his cat, Stripey, and for a few days, me.

He's been great at introducing me to everyone and making sure I get involved in any local expeditions. Around lunchtime today, word came in of a nearby stag sighting and Marcel, a deerstalker from Holland, ran off to get his rifle. Stuart winked and beckoned me to follow.

We caught up with Marcel as he emerged from his house, clad in his camouflage outfit, and headed for his van.

'Is it ok for Rich to tag along?' Stuart asked, 'it'd be good for him to see it.' Marcel looked at Stuart, then at me, then back at Stuart. 'Noooo,' he said, shaking his head, 'I don't think that'd be a very good idea. The stags are very skittish this time of year.'

I wore my disappointed face. So did Stuart.

'I could stay in the van,' I tried, but it was too late. Marcel was off.

An hour later he was back, muttering. He hadn't found the deer. Rum's red deer population stands at about twelve hundred and has been studied at length by various universities on the mainland. As they have now reached maximum numbers, an annual cull of one-sixth of the population is necessary, providing jobs for deerstalkers and pony gillies, two more unusual jobs for outdoorsy people.

Itinerant fishermen and lobster potters also find their way to Rum, giving rise to unusual stories that the locals like to tell and retell at lazy evenings in the village. A few years ago a group of scuba divers brought their van over to Rum for a week or so to do some diving. The strange smell of fish and chips began to pervade the island, most especially when the van drove past. It was particularly surprising out in the high country when a surprised pony gilly or deerstalker would catch a waft of fish and chips in the air. After several days of confusion, it was discovered that the divers were running their van on second-hand cooking oil from a fish and chip shop on the mainland! The mystery was solved.

Insect Girl from Liverpool University is a friendly, heavyset girl with long black hair and an enormous butterfly net. Her name is Jessie. Three months ago she placed a series of insect traps in a small, fenced-off area up in the highlands of Rum. Today, Stuart and I accompanied her to recover her traps. She had her grids all carefully marked out and recorded via GPS which pointed her to the exact spot of each trap. The fact that the trees now had leaves caused her GPS to falter somewhat, and she had to resort to memory. Once the bugs are carefully preserved in alcohol, Insect Girl will begin to make deductions based on the number and type of insect in each trap.

Bloodstone Hill is a series of sheer cliffs on the northern coast of Rum that I thought must hide an interesting past. I was a little mistaken as they were named after a mineral, bloodstone, which is found there.

The west coast of Rum is dominated by sheer cliffs and broad stretches of open ground, covered in rich green grass. It's the perfect hangout for Highland cows, Rum ponies, red deer and goats, but as for human habitation, well, there is none. In the winter time, great storms rage in from the North Atlantic, and the coastline is battered and beaten. Hardly the sort of place to be inhabited by anyone. Except for the goat girls of Na Hearadh that is.

Stuart had a few fences to fix on the west coast this afternoon, and I went along for the ride and found myself clambering about above the sheer cliffs and gaping down at the wild, beautiful scenery. The only sign of habitation was a desolated mausoleum, resembling a mini Acropolis, standing alone on the windswept peninsula, and a small white house standing nearby. The mausoleum contains the graves of John Bullough, and those of his son, Sir George Bullough and Sir George's wife, Lady Monica.

About a hundred metres from the mausoleum stands the house – the home of the goat girls. I had heard a lot about them in the village and wanted to meet them, but they were nowhere to be seen. I followed a few goats for a while, thinking perhaps that they'd lead me to the girls but I was not so lucky.

This part of the island is known as Harris, or Na Hearadh in Gaelic, and two young women, who are referred to as 'the goat girls' in the village, apparently live here on their own, with a small dog, a storm lantern and a fire for comfort, observing their goats. It would have been nice to meet them...

Following the goats into the hills, I came up the crest of a ridge and happened upon the sight of three beautiful red deer stags, grazing peacefully in a little valley. I startled them, and they ran off. Keeping downwind from them and using my best leopard crawl technique, I stalked them for a while and eventually, with just my camera and a bit of my head in sight, got my photograph.

I may not have found the goat girls of Na Hearadh, but as usual, I had stumbled on the unexpected and returned to the village smiling at the thought of those red deer wandering free.

Carelessly, I forgot to mention them to Marcel.

Winklepickers   Fishing.
Goat girls   1200 deer
Deer stalker   1/6 cull
Pony gillies
Castle guides   Fish n Chips
Ratman   Mallaig
Peter, First Warden   Winklepickers

CHAPTER SEVENTEEN

The Goat Girls of Na Hearadh

On the train from Rum
June 18th — 57°00'38.59"N, 6°15'53.05"W

It was time to say goodbye to Rum, and the boat left as it had arrived – with low overhead clouds clinging thickly to the mountain, the castle looking menacing amidst the trees and the surrounding waters choppy and dark. Staring back at the retreating castle and the darkening island, I thought back to Greenland and the chain of events that brought me here. I might have guessed that fate hadn't finished with me.

'Your name is Rich,' a voice at my shoulder told me, and I turned to find a smiling, redheaded girl looking at me. 'Stuart's friend?' she continued.

'Aye,' I said, recognising another redheaded girl walking up behind her as Kate, the girl from the Rum General Store, the one who had been so impressed that I knew Raggi.

'I'm Roz,' said the first girl, laughing and shaking my hand. 'I'm one of the goat girls.'

'Ahh,' I said, my eyes widening, 'I've been looking for you.'

I told her of my search on the green peninsula on Rum's west coast and showed her the goat photographs on my camera. She squealed with excitement, and Kate raised her eyebrows at me in mock protest.

'Aye, that's Mint,' pointed Roz, 'and that's Canna - he's a male kid - he was born in February.' She also identified 'Islay' and 'Shetland' and told me that they'd started naming the goats after islands.

The boat from Rum landed us at Arisaig, where the three of us caught the train on to Fort William. We sat together, and I began to piece together the story of the goat girls of Na Hearadh.

Goat girl number one is Lesley, and she is doing a research project on the several hundred feral (wild) goats on Rum. Lesley spends her days following her goats around, clipboard in hand, recording their movements. Her particular emphasis is an energy study, recording and analysing the different plants the goats are eating and their resultant energy levels. Roz is goat girl number two, and she is Lesley's assistant.

'We met a few years ago on St. Kilda, studying the feral sheep there. 'Ave you heard of St. Kilda?' Roz asked.

I shook my head, my eyes still out on stalks.

'It's the furthest west island that there is,' she said, 'the last land mass before you get to America. When Lesley got the grant for the research on Rum, she phoned me up. They wouldn't let her do it on her own. Safety in numbers, you know. Gets too lonely on yer own anyway.'

I nodded. I could imagine.

'I've got my own wee project too,' she said proudly. She was in top gear, her eyes shining with enthusiasm.

Kate joined in the conversation.

'Has to write down what they do every minute,' she said proudly.

'Every minute?' I stared at Roz in amazement.

'Aye,' said Roz. 'It's fine when they don't go too far, but sometimes they're up in the mountains, and it gets a bit hairy.'

I just shook my head at her, my mouth hanging open.

'It's not so bad,' said Roz. 'We come into the village for weekends, to stock up on food and to party. They call us the goat girls, you know?' she said, forgetting that she'd already introduced herself as such.

'Yes,' I laughed, 'I know.'

Roz and Kate are sisters. Kate had come to visit Roz a few months ago and fell in love with the island and one of the 'keeper of the cows' at the same time. So she stayed.

My time in Rum is over, and I can't help but reflect on these inspiring people I keep finding. They're amazed at me – travelling around and writing it all down. I'm amazed at them – following goats around with a clipboard for months on end, recording every moment. Perhaps we aren't too different after all?

ARISAIG   GLASGOW

CHAPTER EIGHTEEN

Puffins in their Porridge

Glasgow, Scotland
June 21st — 55°51'52.11"N, 4°15'05.31"W

'Ave you heard of St. Kilda?' Roz asked me on the train a few days ago, propelling me into several days of intrigue.

Roz, goat girl number two, met Lesley, goat girl number one, on the group of islands known as St. Kilda two years ago. Unusually, for goat girls, they were both there on sheep business. Feral sheep that is. In fact, they were researching the Soay sheep – small, brownish-coloured wild sheep that live exclusively on the tiny island of Soay, and have done for centuries.

But first, a geography lesson. Off the north-western coast of Scotland, above the Isle of Skye and the Small Isles of Rum, Muck, Eigg and Canna, lie the Western Isles, also known as the Outer Hebrides. These are cold and wintry isles, thirty miles from the mainland, and host to the hardiest of Scotsmen. Fifty miles west of the Western Isles, and bearing the full brunt of the great Atlantic storms, lies St. Kilda – isolated, barren and boasting the highest cliffs and most spectacular island scenery in all of Britain. It is a grouping of three main islands – Hirta, Soay and Boreray – as well as some jagged rocks that spire upwards out of the sea. It is also the home of some of the largest colonies of seabirds – fulmars, gannets and puffins – in the world.

I'd never heard of St. Kilda.

Roz, goat girl number two, sitting opposite me on the train to Fort William, told me the amazing tale of the people of St. Kilda, an independent and separate grouping of people who lived there for many hundreds of years. In 1930, with their numbers dwindling and racked by famine and mainland diseases, they were removed from these inhospitable islands for good, at their own request. It is the story of how they had survived for hundreds of years that bears retelling.

'Their feet had evolved differently to ours,' said Roz, nodding at my frown. 'Yes, their heels were a third thicker, and their toes were curled so that they could climb the cliffs.'

The people of St. Kilda lived off the seabirds that nested there every year. They would kill them in their tens of thousands, and dry and store them for the long winter months. The barely arable land gave them a small harvest of potatoes and oats, but their staple diet was the seabird. They would trade the feathers and oil from the birds with the mainland, but this was only in more recent times.

'They dried out the birds in rock cairns that are still there on the island,' said Roz enthusiastically, recalling her time on St. Kilda. 'It's so beautiful – it's a World Heritage site now.'

The St. Kilda community didn't have a leader. The men would meet each morning in the street outside one of their stone and turf houses and, by consensus, would agree what would be done that day. They called it their 'parliament'. It was the ultimate in socialism. Everything was shared. The daily catch of birds would be divided equally among all the households, no matter who had caught what. Apparently some days the parliament would take all day, and no work would be done. The men loved to talk. In fact, all the men did was catch the birds, ride in the boats and talk. The women did most of the work – carrying heavy things, digging in the fields and tending to livestock. They also fetched water and did all the cooking. The making of clothes, however, was done by the men!

'They really loved the taste of the seabirds – they weren't even that keen on mutton – they preferred the birds,' Roz continued. 'For breakfast, they weren't happy with the taste of their oats, so they would boil a puffin in with their porridge for extra taste,' she said, smiling at Kate and I, our faces all screwed up.

It is an amazing story and a sad one too. Since my train trip with Roz and Kate, I visited Glasgow and searched out a book on St. Kilda, titled *The Life and Death of St. Kilda* by Tom Steel. I have spent the last few days reading about the hard life of these islanders, and how the intrusion of the outside world ultimately brought their demise.

For centuries they were sceptical about contact with the mainland, and resisted any new 'inventions', like using a horse to plough, or a spade, and particularly, modern medicine. Ultimately though, they succumbed and new diseases brought ill health and death, and fancy possessions wrought discord in the community.

In the end, their lives were just too hard, and the few that were left agreed to begin anew in a better place.

They left behind the wild sheep of Soay, and the colonies of fulmars, gannets and puffins that still breed there year after year. The people who visit now no longer go to see the wild people of St. Kilda, but go instead, with clipboards and cameras, people with professions as strange today as the bird people of St. Kilda were a century ago.

boiled puffin

  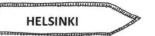

'Balls to the Wall'
The unfortunate Harry

'The Forbidden Isle'
My view of Rum, arriving by boat

'The Forbidden Isle'
Kinloch Castle, on the Isle of Rum

'Raggi of Rum'
The store, the pub, the post office

'The Home of the Original Job'
The stags that Marcel, the deerstalker, never heard about

'The Goat Girls of Na Hearadh'
The Bullough Mausoleum, the Goat Girls' house, and a guard

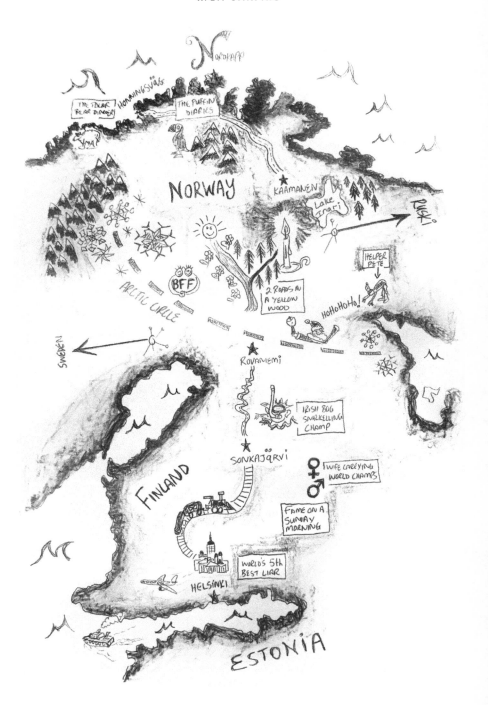

CHAPTER NINETEEN

On My Own Again

Helsinki, Finland
June 23rd — 60°19'15.90"N, 24°57'09.90"E

She was exquisitely beautiful, a fragile face tanned brown, a porcelain doll in bronze. Her hair was white blonde and tied up tightly against her scalp; her physique both slight and strong.

'Immensely Scandinavian,' I thought, staring into her blue, blue eyes.

She stared right back at me, at my own bronzed features, my rough beard and my hazel brown eyes.

'I must be desperate,' I thought to myself, 'chatting up airline staff.'

I found myself at Helsinki domestic airport, several hours early (as is my custom) for my flight north to Rovaniemi. On my way to the Isle of Rum, I read about the strangest event, happening in Finland – the Wife-Carrying World Championships, and that I might be able to meet the real Santa Claus! These possibilities, together with a keenness to get back to cold places, had brought me here, to this particular check-in desk. There was no queue behind me, no one to interrupt this long, drawn-out, delightful check-in.

Her teeth flashed at me, shining white, perfectly formed.

'So many places,' she said, long nails poring through the stamps in my passport. I looked around self-consciously, half-expecting her supervisor to fire her for extravagant time wasting.

She went through the pages one by one, asking my help occasionally when she couldn't decipher a stamp. It was evident that she had been to many of them.

'What are you going to do in Finland?' she asked.

'I'm here to see Santa and his reindeers,' I said, and saw her eyes make a funny expression.

(Note to self – when talking to beautiful women, it's not clever to admit to believing in Santa Claus)

I tried to recover.

81

'Well, maybe just the reindeers. But I'm really here for the Wife-Carrying World Championships.'

She'd never heard of that.

'In Sonkajarvi, in ten days' time – you know, the Wife-Carrying?'

She nodded, but she didn't really know, and I realised she now thought I was married.

I wasn't very good at this, clearly.

I wanted to tell her how much I was looking forward to seeing Lapland and maybe catching a glimpse of a wolf or a moose, but it was too late.

My boarding pass printed out, and she handed it to me with a smile.

'Have a lovely time,' she said, and I was on my own again.

My boarding pass prints out and she hands it to me with a smile.

'Have a lovely time,' she says and I am on my own again.

HELSINKI   SANTA'S VILLAGE

CHAPTER TWENTY

Christmas in June

Santa's Village, Lapland, Finland
June 25th — 66°57'36.79"N, 25°50'47.11"E

In this most northerly part of Scandinavia, in this land called Lapland, where the pine trees form great forests against the grey skies, and where the reindeer wander at will, I found myself at Santa's place, awaiting an audience with this busiest of men. Well, in fact, today, June 25th, was his quietest day of the year, the furthest possible date either side of Christmas. But he had agreed to see me.

'Hello, where are you from?' I heard Santa's elf say to the couple in front of me, waiting at the entrance to Santa's cave. The elf was dressed in a green Robin Hood-looking costume and had a straggly brown beard that looked as if it may have been stuck on. He was in his mid-twenties I guess, but then who knows with elves? A little badge had his name, Pete, printed on it.

'We're from Madrid, Spain,' said the woman, trying to peer past Pete into the cave, where Santa's booming voice could be heard in the distance.

'I knew a Spanish girl once,' says Pete, leaning against the wall, his eyes staring upwards, his mind far away. A strange lecherous look crosses his features.

'I knew a Spanish girl once,' said Pete, leaning against the wall, his eyes staring upwards, his mind far away. A strange lecherous look crossed his features. Naughty elf. Naughty, naughty elf.

While I waited my turn, I read a framed and faded letter hanging on the wall of the cave. It was dated November 18, 1906.

My dear Santa Claus

This is the last year I expect anything from you. This year I wish a Indians feather hat, a bow and arrow, a pair of tites and some grece paint and a tommy hook. I hope that you and the dear old rainders are very well.

With love from Gavin, London

To reach Santa Claus, I had to find my way to Lapland in northern Finland and then, eight miles north of a town called Rovaniemi, in a forest of pine trees, I had to step across a line marking the 66th parallel (in fact 66°32'35"), also known as the Arctic Circle. I then turned to the right, and climbed the wooden steps to 'Santa's Cave', which is near to another wooden building with the sign, 'Santa's Post Office'.

Santa has to date received over ten million letters from children in 187 countries. Last Christmas alone he received five hundred thousand letters. He must be a very busy man. But not today.

'Hello, where are you from?' I heard Pete, the elf, say, and I realised the Spaniards were with Santa.

'I'm from South Africa,' I said. 'Oh,' said Pete. It was clear that he'd never had a South African girlfriend.

We chatted for a while, Santa's elf and I, just small talk about everyday things. I asked where best to find wild reindeer and what time of year they shed their antlers. Pete asked if South Africa was a nice place to live and if there were pretty girls.

From behind me a rude woman bustled past and asked Pete, Santa's elf, how much it cost to have a photograph taken with Santa.

Pete slumped his shoulders a little and said to the woman,

'I am just a simple elf. I am sorry, but I don't know anything about money.' She should have asked him about girls.

Pete ushered me into Santa's lair. To my left, the wall had shelving to the ceiling, giant shelves holding giant books, each book three foot high. One said *Aasia*, another *A-E*, another *Afrikka*. Santa sat comfortably in a big chair by the fire, eyeing me in a friendly sort of way. Behind him on the wall was an ancient map of the world and to the side of him, bags of presents, no doubt for children who were already good!

'Helloooo, how are you?' asked Santa, extending his hand.

I shook it.

'My name is Rich,' I said.

'I'm Santa,' said Santa.

I sat on a metal coffee table on his right, just next to the big Christmas tree. As you might expect he was a big man, dressed in red and with a long white beard that reached his lap.

'Very fine weather we have today,' said Santa.

I didn't know what to say to Santa. For once I was speechless. Should I ask for presents?

'Soon,' he continued enthusiastically, 'soon, it will be snowing.'

I nodded. Enthusiastically, I hope.

'I remember when you were just a boy,' he said, rubbing my leg.

I'd heard of these sort of Santa's.

'Where are you from again?' he asked, struggling to remember from so long ago. 'Port Elizabeth, South Africa,' I said, wondering if he knew where it was.

'Gee,' he said, fiddling with his beard, 'I haven't been there for, let me see ... six months, I think,' he laughed and reached for a great book behind him.

The Book of Presents, I hoped, but no, it was a giant atlas, weather-beaten and dog-eared.

'Port Elizabeth,' mumbled Santa, looking for the page for South Africa. As he thumbed through his atlas, I gazed in amazement at the detailed scribbles and squiggles on each page – children's' names all over the world.

'Welkom,' Santa says suddenly, pointing to the small town in the middle of South Africa. 'Now that is a very nice town. Have you been there?'

'Oh yes,' I say quickly, lying.

One shouldn't lie to Santa.

On the page, next to Welkom, is written in the name 'Rust'.

'Welkom,' Santa said suddenly, pointing to the small town in the middle of South Africa. 'Now that is a nice town. Have you been there?'

'Oh yes,' I said quickly, lying.

One shouldn't lie to Santa.

Written on the page, next to Welkom, was the name 'Rust'.

'Do you know Rust?' asked Santa.

'No,' I admitted, 'I'm afraid I don't.'

'Oh dear,' said Santa, 'well – next time you go there, you give him my regards.'

'I certainly shall, Santa,' I said, a bit sheepishly. I looked at Port Elizabeth in the atlas, and it was empty, blank. No presents for Port Elizabeth.

Santa wrote 'RICH' in big letters next to Port Elizabeth and smiled.

'See you at Christmas,' he said, and we smiled for the camera.

Oh, I've been good. Really, I have.

'Christmas in June'
Tell the truth, Santa. It's all being written down

CHAPTER TWENTY-ONE

A Midsummer Day's Dream

Rovaniemi, Lapland
June 25th — 66°30'14.29"N, 25°44'23.73"E

The Arctic Circle is that imaginary line above which the sun does not rise for at least one day in winter and where you can see the midnight sun on at least one day in summer. Yesterday was that day.

In Finland, it's called Midsummer's Day, and it's the biggest day of the year. The girls wear flowers in their hair, the liquor stores enjoy a brisk trade, and everyone says 'Happy Midsummers'. It's the longest day of the year, and officially, it's the start of summer!

Summer is a happy time for Finns. The weather is warm. It is light all day long. The reindeer are shedding their antlers, and it is holiday time.

I found myself in Rovaniemi, a big, little town in southern Lapland, not far from Santa's forest. Everyone was excited – I could see it in the youngster charging to his mates with a six-pack in hand, the campers arriving en masse along the river and the myriad sounds of celebration wafting to me in my lonely lodgings at a B&B on the edge of town.

What I felt like doing was putting my feet up for the evening, perhaps taking in a movie, but it was like New Year's Eve here, and I felt I should be somewhere special. I took to the streets of Rovaniemi instead, searching for a party. After a while, I heard singing and soon found myself inside a beautiful Lutheran church, joining in a carol's service. All the songs were in Finnish, of course, but strangely, that made it more meaningful. The church's frescoes and paintings incorporated many of the symbols of Lapland – the reindeer, the wolf, and the snow.

After the service, I approached a friendly looking Finnish girl, and she explained that all the songs were about nature and God's love, and how this was such an important part of their religious year.

I asked if there was a Midsummer's party and she pointed me down to the riverside, between two bridges, where I found a series of marquee tents and the sound of accordions playing. It was the annual Rovaniemi Midsummer's Eve Festival, and it began with an official 'Proclamation of the Summer' ceremony followed by traditional folk dancing and the lighting of the midnight bonfire on the river.

I bought a jug of Koff lager, sat myself down near where the salmon steaks and reindeer sausages were sizzling on the open fire and waited to see how the Finns partied. A large circus tent nearby had a huge dance floor around its centre pole, and a four-man band began to play, attracting Finns from all directions. As I carried my beer across to watch the dancing, I felt like I was at some strange combination of a gypsy folk festival, an Irish music hall, and a Russian polka dance.

The Finns amazed me with their dancing. It was all traditional close dancing stuff, and extremely impressive. They were smartly dressed for the occasion and showed off skills that must be a national tradition.

The Finns are renowned for being a quiet, reserved nation, their pale, slim features and blonde hair probably adding to this image, but I saw none of that reservation last night. They were happy and celebrating.

After a dinner of poro pyttis, which is reindeer sausage served with potato and onion, I wandered down to the edge of the Kemijoki River, where another stage had been erected, and a brilliant exhibition of the traditional Finnish polka was given by a group of young Finns.

At midnight a traditional bonfire raft was set alight on the water, to the cheers of everyone, including the people hanging over the bridge and on the opposite bank.

The Arctic Circle has as its function the definition of light and dark in this part of the world. For the Finnish people, today represents a new start, a day of celebrating life – the day when the sun does not set.

Here in Rovaniemi, at midnight, it was a dreamlike scene.

A real wooden house, built on a giant raft, drifted slowly past as the bonfire raged on, while in the sky, the sun still shone just above the horizon and a rainbow welcomed in the summer.

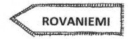  

ROVANIEMI   KAAMANEN forest

CHAPTER TWENTY-TWO

A New Friend

Kaamanen Forests, Lapland
June 26th — 68°54'03.97"N, 27°04'18.71"E

I have a new friend. His name is Paul.

Choosing where to go next is a major challenge when travelling. Or it can be if you get worked up about it. Usually, when one travels with other people, it gets quite stressful, and the final choice gets deliberated upon more than it should. The way I enjoy travelling the most is when some element of chance is attached to the decision. In a big group, this sort of travelling is impossible; it just doesn't work. With two or three of you, if you are compatible and like-minded, it can work. On your own, as long as you are laid-back, it works every time.

Today I found myself stranded in southern Lapland, in Rovaniemi. I knew I wanted to visit Santa and cross the Arctic Circle, but that was now done, and I still had a week's free time before the Wife-Carrying World Championships. Oh, joy. That is the best of feelings. A whole week of random choice. Seven days in the hands of fate.

To guide me in my choice of destination I asked the opinion of a few helpers that I have met along the way. To each of them, I said that I wanted to experience rural Finland and see some wildlife.

'Where should I go?' I asked.

My friendly bus driver yesterday, Michel, who took me to and from Santa's village, was very talkative and suggested I go west towards Raanujarvi, near the Swedish border. He said that there were lots of lakes, and the terrain was 'promising'.

My good friend, Pete, Santa's elf, suggested I go east, to a place called Kuusammo, where there are also a lot of lakes. He didn't specifically mention women but, given his track record from yesterday, I'm somewhat doubtful as to his focus on wildlife.

The lady manning the information desk at Santa's village, Eva-Maria Hiltunen, who was born in Germany, grew up in Australia and married a Finn, and is a personal friend of Santa's, suggested I head into the far north of Finland, near the border of Norway and Russia. 'There're some lovely lakes there,' she said.

In the end, the final decision was made by the bus timetable and I caught the first bus out of Rovaniemi. It happened to be heading north.

It was while waiting for the bus that I met Paul Chung, my new friend. He was also the only other person there. In his mid-twenties, Paul is Korean and has long bushy black hair that sticks out at all angles, giving him the look of permanent surprise. He is short and compactly built, with a little goatee beard and smiles a lot. His English is a lot better than my Korean.

An Australian couple from Perth on the bus north today had some difficulty recognising my South African accent and leaned over and said, 'Glad to see another Aussie on board!'

They have just completed the Trans-Siberian Railway journey, through China and Mongolia and Russia, finishing in Helsinki. It is one of travelling's epic trips, with stopovers in Beijing, in Ulaanbaatar, in Moscow and in St. Petersburg. They spoke of the vastness and wonder of the Gobi Desert, of a dinner under the stars with the nomads of Mongolia and their beautiful horses, and the long ride through Siberia. They also mentioned interminable delays at border posts, inconsistent train standards and a few other moans and groans. Their theory about travelling is that you enjoy it far more later on when you reminisce!

We turned the six-hour bus ride from Rovaniemi to the shores of Lake Inari into a safari by sitting up front near the driver and gazing out the huge front window as we made our way through the great pine and spruce forests of Lapland. All in all, we had six different sightings of reindeer, ranging from a pair in the middle of the road stopping all the traffic, to a great herd on the hillside.

The term 'Lapland' refers to that northern part of Scandinavia, incorporating parts of Norway, Sweden, Finland and Russia, and was the original home range of the Sami people. Lapland seems to consist of either forest or lakes. Even the smaller towns are mostly hidden in the trees. The pine trees, while quite large, do not reach the heights of trees in warmer climes. The long frozen winters here must exact a toll on the growth of the average tree.

The bus dropped Paul and I at a hostel in Kaamanen, near to the huge Lake Inari and, after a few beers, we decided to search the surrounding forests for wildlife, an activity I never seem to tire of.

'How do we decide which way to go?' asked Paul.
In the forest all routes look equally promising.
'What do you do in your country?' I asked.
'In my country,' he said, looking a little embarassed.
'you spit on your hand and then whichever direction it
is pointing, that is where you go!'

'How do we decide which way to go?' asked Paul. In the forest, all routes looked equally promising.

'What do you do in your country?' I asked.

'In my country,' he said, looking a little embarrassed, 'you spit on your hand and whichever direction the spit is pointing, that is where you go!'

I couldn't match that. I took out a dice from a side pocket of my backpack and showed it to him.

'Before I left, my sister gave this to me, to help with choices. I must number my choices one to six and then throw the dice.'

'Ahh,' said Paul, really getting into this. 'Also – in my country – if it is just between two,' he said, his eyes wide beneath his forest of jet black hair, 'then we go – 'I-like-de-li-cious-co-ca-co-la'.

We both laughed a little; I said 'Why don't we go that way?' and we went.

The Lapland forest is a very pretty place to walk. The thin pine trees are close together and it's a struggle for any plant to make it big out here. It's just too cold most of the time. We walked for some time over a meandering path that crossed little streams and patches of open ground but saw nothing. Once, I thought I heard a small bird, but I might have been mistaken. They should come to Africa, the Finns!

About midway through our walk, we came to a place where the path forked into two directions – one clear path and the other not well used.

'Have you heard of Robert Frost?' I asked. Paul looked at me blankly. 'He's an American poet,' I added, ready to begin reciting.

'Two roads converged in a yellow wood,' he said suddenly, smiling and surprising me, 'and I took the one less travelled by,' he continued, and then stopped.

'And that has made all the difference,' I finished, and we laughed, a South African and a Korean quoting American poetry in a Lapland forest!

'And that has made all the difference,' I finished, and
we laughed, a South African and a Korean quoting American
poetry in a Lapland forest!

CHAPTER TWENTY-THREE

Leatherbacks and Jungle Brothers

On the bus to Norway
June 27th — 69°14'18.33"N, 27°14'42.96"E

What would I have in common with a funky Korean dude with big hair and a liking for trip-hop music, whatever that is? Apart from the poetry of Robert Frost and a passion for travel, nothing it would seem.

'You know Jungle Brothers?' he asked me yesterday, smiling and nodding enthusiastically. I returned the smile and nodded uncertainly, but then gave up and said, 'No, is that a movie?'

One thing that Paul Chung and I do have in common is our enjoyment of music. In the spirit of transcontinental goodwill, we swapped iPods for a few hours and submitted ourselves to each other's music. Genres on his iPod included Breakbeat, Classic Rock, Dance, East Coast, Electronic, Funk, Hip-hop, LoFi, Rap, R&B and Trip-hop. His search on my iPod would have given him Blues, Classical, Folk, Country, Easy Listening, Afrikaans, Instrumental, Seventies and Pop, amongst others.

Artists on his iPod included Thelonius Monk, Tuff Crew, Andre 3000, Big Boi, Blackalicious, Bumpy Knuckles, DJ Sushi, Madlib and Bjork. A far cry from my John Denver, Ddisselblom and Rodriguez!

Paul has a most interesting way of travelling. He volunteers for two-week work camps all over the world, at which he gets to do exciting and meaningful things (sometimes) and meets different people from many countries, all at minimal cost.

So far he has done five such camps over the past three years. He's just completed two weeks in central Finland marking out a new hiking trail and leaves shortly for Estonia for a similar project. His most interesting work camp was in Mexico where he worked to save the endangered leatherback turtle. Each night between one and five a.m. they would walk the beaches, searching for turtles arriving to lay their eggs. The turtles are aggressive until they start laying and then they are oblivious to everything, and can even be collared for future monitoring.

Once the eggs are laid, and the leatherback is back in the sea, Paul and his fellow volunteers would carefully steal the eggs and take them to a special hatchery. At the end of his time there, Paul had the thrill of taking a basket of newly hatched turtles down to the sea and releasing them to the safety of the waves.

In other work camps, Paul has helped rid San Francisco of noxious plants and dug manure for an organic farm in the south of France.

Paul and his friends recently started organising funky dance parties in Seoul, and these have mushroomed to over a thousand people each time. Tonight was the largest party yet, and Paul felt very far away.

'You must know DJ Krush?' asked Paul of me in exasperation, desperate to prove that my distance to his generation was not in fact that far.

I looked at him blankly.

'Very famous Japanese DJ,' said Paul sadly.

One thing that we do have in common is the love of travel, and we have spent many hours comparing notes about Thailand, Mexico, Hawaii and other places we have both visited.

Paul and I are now in the process of changing countries. Having travelled together through most of Finland, it has been difficult not to notice that, but a mere one day's bus ride to the north, lies the northernmost point of Europe, the very top of the world perhaps? It is called Nordkapp, or North Cape, and looks out over the Arctic Ocean towards the North Pole. And it is in Norway, where Raggi hails from. It's too close not to make the trip!

So it's the bus to Norway then for my funky friend and me. Sometimes you've just gotta do what you've gotta do.

At least he'll have some decent music to listen to!

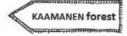  

CHAPTER TWENTY-FOUR

Where Raggi Used to Roam

Nordkapp, Norway

June 28th — 71°09'51.47"N, 25°47'04.26"E

'You do have a campervan, right?' asked the old man wearing a faded white singlet.

Paul Chung and I were stuck at two in the morning in a tiny settlement somewhere south of Nordkapp, the very top of Europe, and were trying to find accommodation for the rest of the night.

'Why would we be looking for a room, if we had a campervan?' asked Paul, exasperated. We'd woken the old man by ringing the bell on the reception desk at a small hotel that didn't look like it would pass any tourism council grading tests.

'Well, it's summer and our rooms are full – always are,' he said, scratching at his chest. 'You should have stayed on the bus.'

Paul and I, fresh from a long bus trip and a lot of funky music, had arrived around midnight at Nordkapp. It felt like the top of the world, a flat-topped peninsula high above the Arctic Ocean, looking out spectacularly towards the North Pole. In old times, it was thought to be the end of the world. It was strange to feel the icy wind coming in from the cold ocean and yet, at midnight, to have the sun above the horizon! We took lots of photographs, and admired a giant steel structure of the globe, and another monument to 'The Children of the Earth'.

We got so distracted that our bus left without us, stranding us on the Arctic, so to speak. We managed to hitch a lift to the next village, where we spotted a hotel sign, and that's where we ran into Singletman, and his helpful advice on campervans.

Out of options, we wandered around a bit, looking longingly at campervans parked beside the road. We ended up around the back of the hotel, where Paul showed his intrepid side by finding an unlocked door to the hotel kitchen. As could be expected, it was deserted and was sterile and cold, dominated by steel.

96

'We're sleeping <u>here</u>?' I said, pointing at the tiled floor.

'Why not,' laughed Paul, acting like he'd done this before. 'There's nobody here!'

With that, he grabbed one of the frying pans hanging down from a cabinet and, wrapping it in his jacket, fashioned himself a pillow for the night. I watched him for a while, then began to follow his lead. I chose my own frying pan, fished around in my backpack for cushioning clothes, climbed into my sleeping bag, and lay down on the tiled floor.

'Well good night then,' I said, and listened to his funny laugh reverberate off the cabinetry.

A few hours later, surprisingly refreshed, and with the perpetual sun glaring off the steel all around us, we awoke, packed away our frying pans and clothes, and fled before Singletman arrived for his morning grill. It probably would have made a better story if we'd slept in and he'd had to chase us out with a broom or a pan.

We found a bathroom, and coffee and bread at a nearby store, and working out the bus timetables, realised that it was time to say goodbye. Paul needed to head south again, to be on time for his work camp in Estonia, and I was resolved to see more of the fjords of Norway. As we parted, I gave him a copy of a travel book I'd written some years before to help him pass the time, and we resolved to keep in touch.

I stood alone at the bus stop for a long time, my tired eyes squinting at the sun, until a voice behind me said, 'I'm so happy to be leaving this f***ing place.'

'Excuse me?' I said, turning around to see a round-faced woman with dark brown hair, holding a suitcase.

'Norway is such a dump,' she said. 'I'm happy to be leaving.'

I chatted to her for a while, and found out that her name was Terri, a Finnish woman in her mid-thirties, and that she was clearly not happy.

As for the place being a dump, apart from the hotel we'd just 'stayed' in, I couldn't have disagreed more. These then are the fjords of Norway, great fingers cut into the land mass by glaciers long ago and now filled with the chilling waters of the Arctic Ocean – a remarkable place populated by a hardy and remarkable people. Just as the Inuits of Greenland earned my admiration for making a living in such a cold and inhospitable climate, so too are the tough Norwegians, their wooden houses all painted in red, their fishing boats at the ready and the fish racks laden with cod, drying out in the long summer sun.

'I don't know what people see in this place,' Terri moaned again, black clouds of gloom drifting ominously above her. She is what one would call a journeyman worker and, although Finnish, has spent the last ten years or so working all over the world, and has been to sixty countries. Four years ago she did fish packing in Norway. This time around she tried her hand at running a B&B. I suspect that her temperament might have acted against her.

'At least the Danes and the Swedes and the Finns will talk to you,' moaned Terri, 'the Norwegians are the most banal people on earth.'

I wasn't putting up with this.

'I've just come from Greenland, and I met a Norwegian girl there who wouldn't stop talking,' I said, and she just muttered to herself, while we both stared down the street, willing the bus to arrive.

The contrast with Raggi was so clear. 'This is after all, where Raggi comes from,' I thought. 'She grew up on the fjords of Norway, no doubt in a village much like this. Raggi, the happy, friendly soul who never stops talking, for whom nothing is too much trouble. This is where Raggi used to roam.'

'I'd like to leave a neutron bomb under this place,' continued Terri with her tirade against the world, not coming close to bursting my bubble. I looked around at the spectacular scenery, the fishing boats at anchor, and my eyes narrowed as my heart hardened against Terri.

'Oh, I'm sure they're not so bad,' I said brightly, as the bus for Honningsväg pulled up alongside. Boarding the bus I sat as far away from Terri as I could. I set my iPod to random, and the third song in was *American Pie*, about a girl who sang the blues…

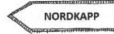

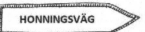

NORDKAPP HONNINGSVÄG

CHAPTER TWENTY-FIVE

The Puffin Diaries

Honningsväg, Norway
June 28th — 70°59'08.40"N, 25°58'53.56"E

A month ago Robbo and I clung to the cliffs of Vik, photographing the puffins of Iceland, and Sigga had tried to get us to eat puffin hearts. Two weeks ago, on the Isle of Rum, I'd been told of a colony of puffins on the nearby island of Canna and was introduced to puffinus puffinus, the beautiful Manx Shearwater. On the subsequent train to Fort William, one of the goat girls had told me of the people of St. Kilda, who would boil a puffin in their porridge to give it flavour. All of these stories have found their way into the pages of my Moleskine notebooks. With the first notebook now full and well-worn, the crisp pages of the second now await new stories.

This afternoon I visited the tiny museum in Honningsväg, and was its only visitor. A young Norwegian guy with a pimply face and long greasy hair offered to show me around, and he soon launched into a boring monologue on the history of the town and showed me a strange collection of old fishing and hunting equipment. At the end of the tour, we came to a large painted mural of an island called Gjesvaerstappen, which is not far from Honningsväg.

'On the fourteenth of April,' said Pimplehead, pointing at the mural, 'one million puffins arrive on Gjesvaerstappen.'

I stopped him right there, not quite hearing him with his strange accent. 'Excuse me,' I said, 'did you say one million puffins?'

He nodded.

'And they all arrive on the fourteenth of April?'

He nodded again.

'Every year the same day?'

He was still nodding. I'm not sure what it is about puffins, but they certainly are following me about on this trip.

The Atlantic puffin is one of three puffin species in the world (although the Rhinoceros Auklet is technically counted as a fourth even though it looks very different). It is the only one found in the Atlantic. It is also known as the sea parrot or 'the clown of the sea', because of its bad flying.

Pimplehead continued.

'On April fourteen, everyone in the town goes out to the island on the boats, between five and six o'clock in the evening, to watch the puffins arrive. The island is a protected area so no one can go on land,' he said, 'but April fourteen is when it all happens.'

> 'So do puffins have diaries then?' I asked pimplehead.
> 'Excuse me?' He looked at me strangely.
> 'Do puffins have diaries?' I asked again, 'You know, so they know when to get here?'

'So do puffins have diaries then?' I asked Pimplehead.

'Excuse me?' He looked at me strangely.

'Do puffins have diaries?' I asked again. 'You know, so they know when to get here?'

Pimplehead looked at me as if I was weird.

'Puffins are birds,' he said, 'just birds,' and left me staring at the mural of the island and wishing that I wasn't two and a half months late.

The species name of the Atlantic puffin is Fratercula Arctica, which in Latin means 'Little Brother of the North.' Given my origins in South Africa and how the puffins keep reappearing on this journey, perhaps they should figure in the title of these notebooks. Reflecting on my time in the museum today, perhaps Pimplehead has inadvertently found us an appropriate title. How does 'The Puffin Diaries' sound?

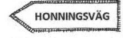  

HONNINGSVÄG · HAMMERFEST

CHAPTER TWENTY-SIX

The Polar Bear Dinner

Hammerfest, Norway
June 29th — 70°39'52.78"N, 23°40'50.59"E

King Harald V, the king of Norway, is also referred to as 'His Arctic Majesty of the Polar Bear.' At least that is what the people of Hammerfest call him.

Arriving by bus from Honningsväg this morning, my spirits recovered after my encounter with Terri and her dark clouds, I spotted two polar bears standing beside the road. They were ceramic, of course, and above them was the sign, 'The Royal & Ancient Polar Bear Society.'

My first destination, naturally, was there.

'Why is it called the Royal & Ancient Polar Bear Society?' I asked the lady at the counter, gazing past her into the dimly lit museum, filled with stuffed animals of all kinds, including a polar bear. She was small, with oversized glasses, but tilted her head down to look at me directly.

'It's a society to preserve the tradition of keeping Hammerfest as a base for Arctic hunting trips,' she said, in the manner of a librarian.

'The polar bear is the town's mascot and heraldic crest,' she added.

Situated near the northern tip of Norway, the town, with its natural harbour and the protected fjord waters nearby, has, for several hundred years, served as a logical starting point for hunting expeditions going north – whales, narwhals and polar bears. While some minke whale hunts are still conducted from these parts, polar bears have been protected by statute since 1973, and narwhals are also wholly protected.

I left the spectacled lady at her desk and wandered through the small museum, realising quickly that this was yet another museum that I had entirely to myself. I was fascinated with the display on Svalbard, a group of Norwegian-owned islands about eight degrees northeast of Norway, which is a very long way. While there are no polar bears on mainland Norway and haven't been for a thousand years, Svalbard has polar bears in large numbers, as well as a variety of other Arctic mammals.

With a start, I realised that I was not alone, for the spectacled lady had appeared almost magically at my side. 'Would you like to buy a polar bear pin?' she asked, holding the small object out to me.

'Oh, no thank you,' I said politely and stepped away a few paces.

'But you must,' she insisted, and followed me, 'you'll never be able to prove that you were here.'

I must have looked puzzled, for she continued. 'These pins are only available here, nowhere else. It's the only way you can say you've really been to the world's most northerly town.'

'In that case,' I said, 'I'll take two,' testing her logic.

'Oh no, sir, we can't do that, only one per person,' she laughed, her laugh ending in a little shriek.

I also asked her why Honningsväg wasn't the world's most northerly town, as I'd just come from there, and it was definitely further north. 'You have to have a minimum of five thousand people to be classified as a town in Norway,' she answered.

I paid for my polar bear, thinking to myself that just as the puffins have seemingly followed me on this trip, the polar bears have not been far behind. I remember the polar bear skin at Kulusuk airport, and hoping not to spot a polar bear during the seal hunt, in case it was shot!

I also received an email this week from none other than Raggi herself, in which she wrote:

Soon after you left, they shot a polar bear here in Kulusuk, and I watched them skin it. I was invited by my new Inuit friend, Manneseq, to join him and his family for a polar bear dinner. It was pretty bizarre. They boil the meat in big chunks with a bit of salt, and you get a plate with a beeeeg chunk of meat and a knife and fork. No vegetables or gravy, nothing, just meat and blubber/fat. I quite enjoyed it. I ate my large lump of meat and the whole family was watching 'Terminator' with Arnie while eating polar bear!

This town of Hammerfest then, where I am now, an industrial looking town in a beautiful setting, is trying hard to position itself in a new world where the hunting of seals, whales and polar bears is becoming increasingly outdated.

The mission of the Royal & Ancient Polar Bear Society is not to save the bears or some similar noble intention, but incredibly, to save Hammerfest. As a final desperate measure to swing the tourist vote their way, they bill themselves as the world's most northerly town, and ration polar bear pins as tightly as passports.

As I said goodbye to the spectacled lady and my money, I walked out past the two ceramic bears, and I wondered about the old days, when the hunting ships returned to Hammerfest, laden with whales and bears, and a spectacled lady rationed out beeeeg chunks of meat, at their own celebratory Polar Bear Dinner.

CHAPTER TWENTY-SEVEN

Interviewing Claus

Santa's Village, Lapland
July 1st — 66°57'36.79"N, 25°50'47.11"E

It had been worrying me for days – remembering that haunted look in the eyes of Pete, Santa's elf, his momentary betrayal of Santa, that instant of uncertainty before he recovered and toed the line again – about reindeers and sunshine and happiness. There had been something there, something deep, something that could not be spoken of. I had sensed it, but its meaning was beyond me. But it had been gnawing at me these past days, days filled with forests and fjords, friendship and funk.

Pete, the elf who belongs to Santa. Pete, the elf with the sad eyes. Pete, the elf who prefers girls to presents. Pete...

Finally, at my wit's end for answers, I returned from Norway and came all the way back to little Rovaniemi. I made my way through the eight miles of pine forests, crossed the Arctic Circle again, made a sharp turn to the right and climbed the wooden steps to Santa's Cave.

'There is too much mystery here,' I thought, 'too much unsaid.' How did Santa deliver all those presents at the same time, how did he know which children were good, where was the mysterious Mrs Claus and what was going on with those elves?

This time I spoke to Santa's PR lady, Leena Nampajarvi.

'I'm a journalist from Africa,' I said. 'I need to interview Santa. I have many questions,' I said in my deepest voice, 'many, many questions.'

After some discussion and checking of schedules, Leena said, 'Santa is having his nap now, but maybe in about an hour?' she asked. So far it all looked above board. They were very accommodating, even nice. Perhaps too nice, my suspicious mind thought in cartwheeling motions for a moment. 'Thank you,' I said, 'but while I wait, would it be possible to speak to Pete?'

'Pete?' she said, looking at me quizzically.

'Pete, Santa's elf,' I said.

'Oh, him,' said Leena, 'of course, of course,' and disappeared into the cave for a moment.

A little later a bleary-eyed Pete was led into where I was sitting. Clearly, Santa's nap was more important than Pete's.

He was surprised to see me again. We chatted for a while, small talk – reindeers and girls, you know the drill – and then, once he was nicely buttered up and ready to turn, I said softly, so that no one could overhear.

'Pete, tell me about the girl elves, their names and what they are like?'

His eyes came alive, his shoulders straightened, and he leaned forward, 'Ahhh, they are wonderful. Maria, Tepso, Marie, they are all wonderful, wonderful,' he said, his bright white teeth shining through his stringy, suspect beard.

'And tell me, Pete,' I said softly, getting ready to delve deeper, 'do you have a girlfriend, a wife?'

'Oh no,' he said sheepishly, 'we are not allowed. And we do not have time, always busy – very, very busy – always is busy.'

He looked around nervously as he said this.

'Too busy for love?' I asked, 'surely not?'

Pete looked at me for a long moment, then I saw the decision in his eyes, and he leaned even closer to me, his face looking down. 'We call them 'special friends',' he whispered, and then looked up into my face, with a knowing smile behind his beard and his eyes wide, wanting a response from me that I understood.

'Ahh,' I said quietly, nodding. 'Special friends,' I said, nodding again. His relief was palpable. It was time to change the subject.

'Tell me about Mrs Claus,' I said, surreptitiously making notes in my Moleskine notebook. I kept eye contact as much as possible. 'I'm getting somewhere here,' I thought to myself.

Pete's eyes shone with respect and admiration. 'Mama Claus,' he said, 'she is wonderful, wonderful.'

'Her cooking,' he continued, putting his fingers to his lips and kissing them, 'her cooking, her rice porridge, it is wonderful, wonderful.'

'What else does she cook?' I asked Pete, expecting a long list.

'Oh no, just porridge, lots of porridge, great pots of porridge for all the worker elves. Sometimes we get her Christmas cookies, and at our big Christmas party she makes the salmon.' He lifted his eyebrows and made as if to swoon at the thought of the delicious salmon.

105

The haunting I have lived through this past week was coming together now, into black and white. I had not imagined it last week – that look in Pete's eyes – that wish, that underlying desire. I needed to speak to Santa. Hundreds of elves working long, long hours to meet impossible schedules, fed only with porridge, day after day, year after year, forbidden to love, resorting to stolen moments with 'special friends'. This couldn't be right.

Pete escorted me to the waiting area for Santa. While we stood there, making small talk, a line formed behind us, and a thin lady with messy hair asked how long she'd get with Santa. 'Oh, just a few minutes,' I replied, not thinking about Pete standing next to me.

He looked at me strangely. 'I'm Santa's little helper,' he said with a wry grin, 'and you're my little helper!'

As he showed me in to see Santa, Pete winked at me. I was flooded with confusion – was it a good luck wink, or did he want something more? Did special friend mean anybody? What was going on here?

Santa was sitting in the same chair as when I'd seen him so briefly last week. This time it was different. He knew I had questions that needed answering. His eyes betrayed him as he felt the firm grip of my handshake. Answers Santa. Answers.

I started slowly. 'Do you ever get presents, Santa?' I asked, my notebook and pen ready.

'Oh yes,' he admitted quickly, 'many presents,' he said, pointing up onto the mantelpiece. 'When people come from far away, they often bring presents.' I could see a fancy clock, a strange, mounted animal resembling a warthog, and some candles. 'Hardly evidence of corruption,' I thought to myself.

I changed the subject, not able to bring myself to confront him on the elves. 'Given your, um, size,' I said, 'how do you manage to fit into all the chimneys at Christmas time?'

He answered, 'Well, I'm Santa Claus, of course.' He looked at me firmly, over the rim of his spectacles. 'It's a kind of magic,' he said, then sort of changed the subject. 'But not in all the countries I visit do I use the chimney. In Finland, for example, I arrive on Christmas Eve and knock loudly on the door. When someone opens I call out, 'ARE THERE ANY GOOD CHILDREN HERE?' And you'll be surprised how often the answer is 'YES, YES, YES!''

In my Moleskine notebook, I had jotted down lots of questions for Santa. At a loss for words, I dived in and chose one.

'What do you do for holidays, Santa?' I asked.

'Well,' he answered, 'what I'm doing is not really a job – why would I need a holiday? If I want to get away, I just get out into nature, take a walk in the forests, swim in the lakes....' He drifted off, his mind far away in some forest, perhaps with Mama Claus, or Pete?

I asked about his favourite foods left for him by children on Christmas Eve. He told me that while he always enjoyed porridge, he preferred to have the national dish of whatever country he was visiting. 'For example,' he said in his funny Finnish accent, 'in England, my favourite is the mince peas.'

'The mince peas?' I asked, confused.

'Yes,' said Santa, 'the mince peas.'

It was time for me to move on to more controversial stuff.

'How can you be in so many places at one time?' I asked, and he nodded slowly and leaned back in his chair, still nodding. It was a question he'd been expecting.

'Well, you see,' he began, 'this was a very real problem for us. One day I went to my doctor friend, Albert, and I said to him, 'Albert, I have so less time, so less to do.' Albert was thinking, thinking, thinking. Then one day he comes back to me and says, 'Santa, I know the solution.' He made me go close to him and whispered in my ear, 'Time is Relative.''

Santa looked at me sternly from under his white eyebrows.

'Ahh,' I said, not clever enough to understand him completely, 'Time is Relative.'

The interview was drawing to a close; my mind was muddled with so many facts, so many questions – about Santa but also about Pete. The lines of children waiting to see Santa were forming outside again and Pete was battling to hold them back. I asked my final question, about the elves and their special friends.

Santa was vague, his mind elsewhere. 'Well, we do not really have rules,' he said and drifted off. The interview was over.

Afterwards, I sat quietly near Santa's Post Office, trying to make head or tail of what I had seen and heard:

Pete, Santa's elf, desperate for special friends and little helpers, and stuffed with porridge and hard labour. Mama Claus, reclusive and captive – cooking, cooking, cooking. Rudolph, the reindeer with the bloody nose. And Santa, forgetful and sleepy, fobbing off interrogation with foibles about magic and advised by the mysterious Doctor E, the man with Nobel-sized solutions.

My mind drifted towards darker thoughts. But dark thoughts about Santa do not last long. I remembered his kind eyes, his soft, forgetful nature and the mince peas. It was time to move on.

Sometimes not all questions have easy answers. Perhaps just believing in the power of good is enough. And getting presents.

CHAPTER TWENTY-EIGHT

The Wife-Carrying World Championships

Sonkajarvi, Finland
July 3rd — 63°40'17.90"N, 27°31'19.51"E

'Our mission,' said the man in a big hat, 'is, in the midst of all the bad news about terrorism and so on, to offer the world one bit of good news.' He paused and looked around the room, filled with journalists and a few hangers-on. 'This is,' he added, 'in honour of all the ladies of the world.'

It was that time of year again. The little town of Sonkajarvi, a rural town in central Finland, in a throwback to the centuries-old practice of stealing women from neighbouring villages, was once again hosting the Wife-Carrying World Championships.

The competitors had come from far and wide. Brandon Ronson and Jenny Aspden were the North American champions and had arrived with banners, flags and t-shirts, and the weight of a continent's expectation. Ian Walker and Sarah Hardingham, from Salisbury in England, were nobody's champions and entered themselves on the Internet. The extent of their practice was 'a romp around our hotel room last night'. Los Eukonkantos I and II were two Finnish couples dressed up, the men seemingly as Laurel and Hardy, the women as 'Heidi' girls. There was a team from Ukraine, about ten more from Finland, a team from Ireland and then there were the Estonians.

Estonia, for those of us geographically challenged, lies to the southeast of Finland, separated by eighty kilometres of the Baltic Sea. Like all good neighbours, a healthy rivalry has developed over the centuries, and it is no more keenly demonstrated than here at the Wife-Carrying World Championships. Whereas the organisers emphasise the fun and spirit of the event, the three Estonian teams place their emphasis on winning and have done so for several years.

First prize is a trophy and the woman's weight in beer! It was perhaps this second part of the prize that attracted the attention of Julia Galvin, one half of the Irish team and on her own probably accounting for one half of the entertainment and spectacle of these entire championships! Since first appearing at the event last year, Julia has slimmed down by twenty kilograms and hit the scales this year at a much reduced one hundred and seventeen kilograms. In her quest for a similar weight in beer, she enlisted the help of last year's All Ireland Arm-Wrestling Champion, Stephen Gracey, a giant of a man, rippling with muscle and tattoos and weighing in at an identical weight to hers.

There were several thousand people gathered for the big event, many of them drinking Olvi lager and eating muikkuannos, which is a pile of sardines, crisply fried in butter and served in a small cardboard container. The crowd was expectant, buzzing, shouting out messages to their favourite competitors, waving flags and grinning stupidly. They sat and stood in makeshift grandstands that surrounded a school's modified athletics track. In the middle, there was a confusion of competitors, organisers, photographers and journalists, a weighing machine to check the 'wives', a podium for the winners and a barrel-shaped, one-man sauna – another prize for the winner.

The track itself was 253.5 metres in length and featured three 'obstacles' – two dry ones, being one metre high hurdles constructed out of logs, and a wet obstacle, a deep plastic-lined pool that was a little over a metre deep and about six metres long.

The 'wife' did not need to be one's own, although there was a category for married or cohabiting couples. There was a formal weigh-in ceremony before the big race, as the woman had to have a minimum weight of forty-nine kilograms; otherwise, she was burdened with bricks!

'It's your turn, Julia,' called one of the organisers of the weigh-in, and Julia stepped forward, dressed in black tights, black t-shirt inscribed with juliagalvin.com, an enormous green leprechaun hat and the Irish flag trailing behind her. The crowd roared their approval, and she gave them a big smile and grabbed the microphone from the surprised announcer.

'Hello Sonkajarvi, I love you,' she called, waving an arm in the air.

There are two distinct styles of Wife-Carrying. The traditional way, piggyback style, is self-explanatory and more, shall we say, dignified, for the woman. The international style, developed by the Estonians in their quest for world domination, is now widely used by anyone interested in personal bests and competitive advantage. It involves the man bowing before the woman (a good start) and the woman lying forward onto his back, her legs trailing either side of his head. As the man stands up, the woman hooks her legs around his neck and grips her hands onto a heavy belt he wears around his waist.

'I have to use the piggy back method,' Julia had said to me earlier, 'Otherwise I just slide off at an angle - I'm a bit top heavy,' she had laughed.

'I have to use the piggyback method,' Julia had said to me earlier, 'otherwise I just slide off at an angle – I'm a bit top heavy,' she had laughed.

After all the build-up, it was race time. The man in the big hat got the crowd nicely worked up, calling out cheers for the different nationalities competing. The cheers for the Finns were naturally the loudest, but the Irish (Julia) weren't far behind!

The competitors were sent off two teams at a time and, after a stumbling jog of about thirty metres, they arrived at the formidable water obstacle. The Estonians and a few of the Finnish couples negotiated it with ease, starting with a practised leap into the pool, then a steady walk and ending with a graceful exit. None of them incurred the fifteen-second penalty for dropping their partner. For everyone else, it was chaos. Ian and Sarah, the novices from Salisbury, seemed to lose balance at the moment of entry and Sarah hung on for dear life, her body at a peculiar angle and her head upside down beneath the water. The crowd was beside themselves with laughter, the photographers clicked away on their Nikons, and Ian forced out a strained grin, his plastic Viking helmet floating beside them. From the side of the pool came their salvation, a big man in an orange diving suit, complete with oxygen tank, goggles and snorkel and he made a big show of checking whether Sarah was still breathing.

After an age, it seemed, they emerged from the water, but their world championship dreams remained behind in the heaving waters of the pond. The Los Eukonkantos couples, the 'Laurel and Heidi's', were paired together and quickly discarded any pretence of contest and bomb-dropped their way into the pool before stealing two luggage trolleys and wheeling their wives up the main stretch, to the screams of the massing crowd. They were, of course, disqualified.

Julia and Stephen, held back to near the end by the organisers, saving the best for last, received a great cheer as they began their quest for the beer and tumbled into the pool with an almighty splash, separating immediately and doggy-paddling the rest of the way. Once out the other side, there was a protracted remounting, with cameras flashing all around before Stephen began his carry for the remaining two hundred metres. At each of the two log hurdles they separated again – there was no other way – before the crowd brought them home. At the finish line, Stephen collapsed on his back, to a great roar of appreciation from the crowd, while Julia stood above him and placed one foot on his stomach and, with both arms raised, gave her triumphant salute. They were last, in a time of 3 minutes and 17 seconds.

Of the others, Brandon and Jenny, the North American champions, took it slowly through the water and tired near the end, finishing ninth in 1 minute and 21 seconds. Ian and Sarah, in a finish that the Vikings would be proud of, broke the two-minute barrier with 1 minute 59 seconds and an overall fourteenth place.

Taisto Miettinen and Eija Stenberg, of Finland, delighted the home crowd with the time of 1 minute and 5 seconds, but their hopes were dashed when the very last couple out, the Estonian pair of Madis Uusorg and Inga Klauson, beat their time by just one-tenth of a second.

I could see the disappointment on the faces of the organisers. They were beginning to take the competitive nature of the Estonians personally! Yesterday afternoon, in the relay version of the same event, the Estonians had finished third and fourth behind two Finnish teams. The Estonians lodged a double objection which, hours later, was upheld by the organisers, and the two Finnish teams were relegated to third and fourth place.

At today's final press conference, the winning wife-carrying team of Madis and Inga were interviewed by the media. Madis, stern-faced, said he was a student and a 1500-metre and 800-metre runner back home. He was also the brother of last year's winner. Inge, who weighed 48 kilograms plus one brick, admitted to playing tennis occasionally.

Julia, having gate-crashed the press conference, called loudly from the back, in her broad Irish accent.

'Do you have any advice for the Irish team for next year?'

Madis looked at her shyly. He didn't know what to say.

'You could lose twenty kilograms,' he said, unfortunately.

Cedric, a French photojournalist, sitting beside me and wearing a jacket with loads of pockets, came to the rescue.

'You're eighteenth in the world,' he said to Julia, 'that's not bad.'

Everyone laughed, and Julia piped up, 'Well, we did a lot better than last year. A whole minute faster.'

And that's the story of the Wife-Carrying World Championships of Sonkajarvi. It was a media event of some magnitude here, attracting strange and unusual entries from all parts of the globe. Some took it more seriously than others, I dare say, but I think that the ones who will be remembered most are those that were here for the fun of it.

I remember one particular incident at the start of the championships. Someone showed Julia the cover of the highlights DVD from last year. She was on the front cover, in all her splendour. In smaller photos on the back were some of the winners.

'Hey, you guys,' Julia called to the Estonians standing underneath their flag. She waved the DVD box at them gleefully.

'You guys might have won. But guess who made the front cover?'

CHAPTER TWENTY-NINE

The Irish Bog Snorkelling Champion

Sonkajarvi, Finland
July 3rd — 63°40'17.90"N, 27°31'19.51"E

Six years ago, Julia Galvin lay in a hospital bed in Ireland, hugely overweight and incapacitated by two slipped discs in her back. She could not walk. Her operation was scheduled for that day. For some obscure reason, she was reading the Guinness Book of Records and found out about the strange and peculiar sport of Bog Snorkelling.

The bog in question is a dirty, smelly trench in the middle of a Welsh peat bog, near a place called Llanwrtyd Wells. Each year, at the end of August, about a hundred entrants arrive, clad in mask, snorkel and fins, and negotiate two lengths of the sixty-yard trench.

Julia read the paragraph about the bog snorkelling, and a strange feeling came over her. 'I'm going to do that one day,' she said to herself.

The next year Julia arrived at Llanwrtyd Wells, a larger than life figure in more ways than one. Her enthusiasm and love for life are infectious, her mood is bouncy and carries no air of falsehood. She is interested in the people she meets, and once she knows you well, I imagine, she is a friend for life.

She made a name for herself at the Bog Snorkelling World Championships in her very first year and has been back every year since. They refer to her as the Irish Bog Snorkelling Champion, although this is a title earned by renown rather than competition. Her email address begins with 'bogchick'.

I was sitting at lunch with Julia, just a few short hours before her appearance in the Wife-Carrying World Championships. We were in the dining hall with all the other participants and the press.

'I won't be making the bog snorkelling this year,' she said sadly, a little miserable at breaking the six-year streak. 'And why not?' I asked, twisting my head away from the remains of my pasta and coleslaw.

'I'm doing the World Mountain Bike Bog Snorkelling Champs instead,' she laughed, and I nearly choked. 'The what?' I said, incredulously.

'The World Mountain Bike Bog Snorkelling Championships,' she said again, evidently pleased with herself at my reaction.

Similar to the regular bog snorkelling, it is an 'under mud' cycling contest, using a snorkel, face mask, and a specially prepared mountain bike which has its tyres filled with lead and water!

'Have you done any other crazy contests?' I asked Julia, pushing my chair back, leaving my food.

'I've done the All Ireland Whistling Champs and the All Ireland Stone Throwing Competition,' she said with a smile, 'and been the length of Ireland in a mini,' she added.

Each day now, I am realising more and more that it is a strange world out there, a world filled with crazy contests and even crazier competitors. In Finland alone, apart from the Wife-Carrying, they also host the World Ice Swimming Championships where a twenty-five-metre long hole is cut in the ice on a frozen lake and competitors have to swim two lengths without the aid of a wetsuit or heat-sealing grease. The Swamp Football World Championships is another Finnish event as is the Mosquito Killing World Championships. In this latter event, competitors go bare-chested into a swamp in mid-summer and see how many mosquitoes they can squash on their torso. And, perhaps in tribute to Nokia, the country also plays host to the Mobile Phone Throwing World Championships!

Julia Galvin is, by profession, a substitute primary school teacher. 'I like the flexibility,' she says, 'I can choose when I want to work.' She lives in the little town of Listowel, in the county of Kerry, on the west coast of Ireland. Her exploits as a bog snorkeler were written about in the Irish papers and the journalist wondered in his article what she would be up to next. 'The Wife-Carrying World Championships, perhaps?' the journalist wrote, giving Julia the idea. However, the problem of finding someone big and strong enough to carry her was not easy to solve. She placed adverts in local Irish papers, and became the butt of jokes of a late night talk show for many a month!

Eventually, in desperation, she called the Irish Strongman Association and was put in touch with Paul Roberts, who carried her last year. This year, Paul was not available but offered to find a replacement, and that was Stephen Gracey, who Julia says proudly, 'He is much bigger than Paul – he's the third strongest man in Ireland and the thirtieth strongest man in the world.'

They only met the day before they flew to Finland.

During the weekend I spent a bit of time with Stephen, struggling manfully to understand his rich Belfast accent. He is a rock of a man, over six foot tall and as solid as concrete. On his right shoulder is a large, circular tattoo that reads, *Train hard or f*** off*. If I ever met him in a dark alley, I suspect I would bash my head against the wall until I passed out. Just to save him the trouble, you know.

Julia convinced Stephen to carry her, although he did admit that, 'I thought Julia was fourteen stone, not seventeen stone.'

After the race, I went up to congratulate them. Stephen was squatting on the ground, physically spent, his vest drenched, his giant shoulders heaving. Julia and I looked down at him, sharing a little laugh. He looked up at us both and glared. 'It's not even funny,' he said in his broad accent, and then, after a moment of panic on my part, smiled.

I am not sure where Julia will turn up next. She is the type of person that you want to see again. At the end of the championships, I went to say goodbye to her, and she gave me a big farewell hug.

As I walked off, she called after me.

'Rich, have you heard the shortest poem ever written?'

'No,' I said, walking back to her, smiling.

'It's titled, *The person you told me to look up in Bahrain said*: and the poem is: *Who?*'

I laughed, she laughed, and I left her.

CHAPTER THIRTY

Fame on a Sunday Morning

Sonkajarvi, Finland
July 4th — 63°40'17.90"N, 27°31'19.51"E

In my hotel room in central Finland, I opened the Sunday morning paper, and my photograph stared back at me. It was a shock, I admit. Rather a big shock. It was quite a nice photograph really. I was wearing a white long-sleeved shirt that didn't look wrinkled and shabby, and my head shone up rather well. 'All in all, I look quite respectable,' I said to myself. Under the photograph, it said, *Afrikasta napapiirille. Rich Shapiro keraa materiaalia matkakirjaan*, which roughly translates to: *From Africa to the Arctic Circle. Rich Shapiro collects material for a travel book.*

There was a nine-paragraph article on me.

Etelaafrikkalainen freelance-kirjoittaja Rich Shapiro tuli Sonkajarvelle huumorin perassa ja tutustumaan mielenkiintoisiin ihmisiin, it began, which translates to: *The South African freelance author Rich Shapiro came to Sonkajarvi in search of humour and to explore interesting people.*

I wandered down to breakfast a little later, wondering if anyone would recognise me. I sauntered over to the fruit section and casually looked around, hoping to catch a furtive glimpse from someone. Nothing. I tried getting a coffee in front of a whole bunch of people, but they didn't even register. Grumpily, on this my birthday of all days, I sat down to breakfast, placing the newspaper strategically on the table. Just in case. I didn't want to be ignored on my birthday. I dragged out my meal, but no one paid me any attention. Afterwards, I wandered up to the reception desk and finally, I got a big smile.

'Helloooo,' said the blonde, giving me that look. You know. Well, maybe you don't if you've never been famous. But it's a look. It's recognition that you can see a mile off. This morning, I was famous! Not in the breakfast room, but at reception...

But before I get ahead of myself let me go back to the beginning.

While en route to the Isle of Rum, I read a small story about the Wife-Carrying World Championships in Finland. I followed up online and sent the organisers an email.

I'm a travel writer and would like to visit your championships in July.

Within the hour I had my invitation, my press accreditation, my hotel details and promises of much to follow. 'Not bad,' I thought to myself.

It got better.

On Friday morning, my backpack and I arrived by train from Rovaniemi, to be met by a beautiful young Finnish girl called Johanna, who promptly said, 'Welcome to Sonkajarvi, I will be your driver and guide this weekend. If there is anything that you need, please ask.'

When they checked me into a fancy hotel, I began to realise that they might have overestimated my journalistic skills and reach just a trifle. When I arrived at the event centre which was a local high school converted for the weekend, Johanna guided me past all the riff-raff, and we followed the signs for *Press* and *No Entry – Press only* and finally, *Press room*. Several times I struggled to suppress a little smile.

There were many introductions, free pencils, free lunch tickets, free everything. I was the sole African journalist, I was told. Before I had taken a breath, I was in the interview room, not interviewing participants, but being interviewed myself. 'What is a South African journalist doing in Finland?'

My answers, I expect, formed the basis of this morning's article in the local Sunday papers.

On Friday evening, I attended a welcome function held in a Finnish forest beside a beautiful flowing river. The press and all the foreign competitors were invited. The local Finnish women, all in their traditional outfits, prepared our welcome dinner which included smoked salmon and a delicious dish that I believe was salmon baked inside brown rye bread. Because the following day was the big competition, no alcohol was served. As could be expected, we press guys were a little disappointed! Before the dinner, they gathered us together by the lakeside in a cloud of vicious mosquitoes and officially welcomed us, and told us that they were treating us to a special event, 'rabbit shooting'.

'This is a bit unexpected,' I thought as we followed them along a windy path near the river, eventually finding several wooden boats tied up alongside the river, and a pile of life jackets and crash helmets. 'Rapid shooting,' I realised with a smile.

It was a grand evening, meeting all the foreign competitors, most especially Big Julia from Ireland, Brandon and Jenni, the North American champions, and Ian and Sarah, the no-hopers who entered on the internet.

Saturday came, and my sojourn in the world of hard journalism continued, fighting my way (with my press pass) into the scrum of photographers beside the water obstacle, my tiny camera looking suspicious alongside those of Reuters and the international press. Later I found myself doing impromptu interviews and joining in the press conferences, chewing my pencil knowledgeably at the back of the press hall, and now and then throwing in a question in my broad South African accent.

And every time I wanted to go back to my hotel, there was Johanna, or Anna, or Katya, ready to do my bidding. Journalism could quickly become my new favourite career!

In just four days, I have interviewed Santa Claus and Pete, his frustrated elf, I've covered my first world championships, and been wined and dined and driven, in true Finnish style. And now, come Sunday morning, I'm the one in the papers...

Sonkajarvi — HELSINKI

CHAPTER THIRTY-ONE

The World's Fifth-Best Liar

Helsinki, Finland
July 6th — 60°09'47.32"N, 24°56'43.33"E

He lectures psychology at the University of Bath. He has a Bachelor of Science, with honours, and a Doctorate in Philosophy (Psychology) from the University of York. His doctoral thesis was the role of language processing mechanisms in verbal short-term memory.

Among his published papers are differences in processing of nouns and verbs in the human brain, a comparison of dyslexic language-impaired children as adolescents, and, drivers' interpretations of a cyclist's gaze and arm signals in a simple judgement task.

He currently lives in a canal boat in Salisbury, which he recently purchased. Unfortunately, shortly after taking possession of the boat, he managed to fall overboard, dislocating his shoulder in the process. At some point in his past, he played the guitar and sang in a three-man band called *The Fat Twins*.

This morning, as I was walking along a random street in downtown Helsinki, the capital of Finland, listening to ABBA music through my earphones, I felt three sharp taps on my shoulder.

'Rich,' said a short girl of about thirty with blonde hair, 'we spotted you from the coffeehouse – are you free for a coffee?'

It was Sarah, from the wife-carrying, and through the window, grinning like the proverbial Cheshire, was Ian.

I met them on Friday evening, at the welcoming function in Sonkajarvi. I had been chatting with Brandon and Jenny, the North American champions, and found myself playing 'the big introducer'. Brandon was very serious, explaining to me how he and Jenny had finished second in the Canadian championships and then when the winners couldn't make it to the North American champs in Maine, they got their chance, which they took with both hands, and qualified to come to Finland.

'How did you qualify?' Brandon had asked the English couple on the other side of me.

Ian, the prospective wife carrier, a mid-thirties bloke of average build, gave Brandon a happy, carefree smile, showing lots of teeth, and said, 'Oh, just in the round-the-lounge-room competition.'

Brandon looked confused. So did I. Sarah came to Ian's rescue.

'We just entered on the internet,' she said. Beside her, Ian nodded happily. He's a very happy guy.

This is what confuses me about Doctor Ian Walker, of Salisbury, England. He has a bumbling, happy-go-lucky way about him. He has a smile that occupies his whole face, takes control of it and gives you – the recipient of the smile – the warm feeling that here is someone who is delighted to see you. It's that sort of smile. He doesn't look like a doctor or someone who spent seven years studying psychology. (A dark thought did cross my mind – 'unless he is really good at it'). He looks much more like a genial plumber, or perhaps an aspirant keeper of the cows on the Isle of Rum.

Brandon and Jenny had lost interest in this increasingly mad sounding couple from England, and I was left alone with them.

'So have you done much practising for tomorrow?' I asked. 'Do you know what you're in for?'

'No, we haven't,' said Ian seriously, in his middle England accent, 'we didn't want to over train, you know,' he said with a wink. 'We want to peak at the right time.'

'We did try it out on a beach a few months ago,' Sarah piped up, and they both laughed at the distant memory.

'And we did have a run around our hotel room last night,' Ian added.

At the race itself on Saturday, they both looked distinctly nervous. 'Oooh Ian, I'm so nervous, I think I've changed my mind,' I'd overheard Sarah say to Ian in jest. But they kept their sense of humour and did the race with a smile, except for a momentary lapse in the pool where Ian's Viking helmet went flying and Sarah remained upside down under the water for longer than she should. But it was a success – the crowd cheered them on. They broke the two-minute barrier and came fourteenth overall.

And so I sat with them both in a coffee shop in central Helsinki, a chance and extraordinary meeting. They asked about my life, genuinely interested. I asked about theirs, even more curious.

'For some time now,' Ian said, 'I've been keen to enter a world championship, get a world ranking at something, you know?'

I nodded, the three of us hunched around the litter of cups on the table. 'Most world championships are really hard to get into,' he continued, 'and too much hard work.'

There's more I haven't told you about Ian Walker.

While not the most athletic of world championship competitors, he does possess a zeal that is not easily overcome. A few years ago he cycled 3600 kilometres from England to the Black Sea and this last Easter he cycled the length of Britain, from John O'Groats to Land's End. He has also walked the 270 miles of the Pennine Way in the north of England.

In his quest for a world ranking, last year he entered the World Lying Championships, which were held in a local pub somewhere in England. With his five-minute story about his career as a tea-bag weaver, he was awarded fifth place, and an official world ranking! Over the dregs of his coffee in the Helsinki coffee shop, he admitted:

'I don't like training, or preparation – very boring,' he said.

'If I'd just prepared for the Lying Championships, I might even have won. I'd be the World Champion now,' he said, staring off into space.

We spent a happy hour together in the Helsinki coffee shop before we swapped email addresses (and details of his website) and went our own ways. Ian insisted that next time I'm in England, I must come and stay on his boat.

Later, in a nearby internet café, I visited Ian's website and found news of his participation in the Wife-Carrying championships:

BATH LECTURER GOES TO WORLD WIFE-CARRYING CHAMPS

The University of Bath's proud tradition of producing world-class athletes is set to continue as Ian Walker, a lecturer from the Psychology Department travels to Finland to compete in the World Wife-Carrying Championships.

'Many people dream of representing their nation in an international sporting competition,' said Ian, 'but then choose sports like athletics and tennis, which require lots of skill and years of training. Big mistake. It's much easier to find a sport that lets absolutely anybody enter its world championships and save yourself all the effort.'

Sarah was also quoted in Ian's press release.

'We're going to get thrashed by the Estonians anyway. They take it very seriously, and their team is a huge guy and a tiny woman. But it'll be fun to take part and uphold our country's great tradition of losing at sports with style.'

As I left the internet café, and made my way down the street, reconnecting with my ABBA music, I marvelled at chance meetings, and fate, and interesting people.

'A Midsummer Day's Dream'
The Midnight Bonfire in Rovaniemi, Finland

'A New Friend'
Paul Chung, from South Korea, in a Finnish forest

'Where Raggi used to Roam'
Rich on the Arctic Ocean, at Nordkapp in Norway

'The Polar Bear Dinner'
The Royal & Ancient Polar Bear Society, Hammerfest, Norway

'Interviewing Claus'
Special friends?

'The Wife-Carrying World Championships'
Julia stands triumphant at the end of the race

CHAPTER THIRTY-TWO

Into the Land of Pink

Hamilton, Bermuda
July 11th — 32°17'40.50"N, 64°47'09.20"W

It has been a long time since I have not had to try to darken my room before going to sleep. In Greenland and Iceland, there was perpetual light. In Lapland and Norway, the sun shone twenty-four hours a day. The effect of this on the human body is rather strange, for one has no idea what time it is when you wake up. Sometimes I would be awake at five thirty in the morning, and on another day I would be amazed to only wake up at eleven. Late at night, perhaps nearing midnight, I was often confused by my body's weariness, only to realise, of course, that it was not five in the afternoon.

Following my new fascination with puffins, I've set a longer-term goal of reaching Alaska, which has two different puffin species and, if you can believe it, another Santa Claus, this time in a town called 'North Pole'. Jacky, my girlfriend from South Africa, has managed to secure a few weeks' leave to join me for the Alaska leg. To get there, I've opted for a few days in a much warmer location, Bermuda, and to then go via New York to Vancouver to meet Jacky and find a cruise ship to take us to Anchorage.

Here in Bermuda, I've met up with my niece Caroline, and her husband, Craig, who recently moved here, and I have been enjoying the dark nights and almost oppressive heat and humidity of the days. I am also enchanted by this elongated island, placed as it is, all on its own, in the middle of the vast Atlantic. A geography lesson was necessary for me to understand exactly where I was, for I had the vague notion that Bermuda was somehow part of the Caribbean.

In fact, it is not near to the Caribbean at all, being a thousand miles to the northeast, and the closest coastline is that of North Carolina, some six hundred and fifty miles away. It lies in the North Atlantic, and its warm seas, its climate and its coral reefs are thanks to the warming effect of the Gulf Stream. Volcanic eruptions millions of years ago formed a large circular island, which over the millennia has reduced to a much smaller, twenty-two mile long, fishhook-shaped island, or series of islands. There are about one hundred and fifty islands in the grouping, some no larger than a boulder.

The islands were uninhabited when stumbled upon by the Spanish sea captain, Juan de Bermúdez, in 1503, and over the centuries the island's reefs have claimed dozens of ships, often resulting in the survivors taking refuge on the island. This was how the British, under Admiral Sir George Somers, first came to the island in 1609, and they later encouraged British settlers and included Bermuda as part of their colonial holdings. In time, slaves from Africa and elsewhere were brought here, and their descendants became the majority of the Bermudans on the island today, going through their own struggle for freedom. Bermuda is an independent country, still tied to Britain, with their own government and prime minister, and with the Queen as head of state.

The island is rich in vegetation and its elongated shape and two huge sounds, where the sea is nearly trapped inside, make for panoramic vistas at every turn. The people are exceedingly friendly and speak with an accent that is strongly West Indian, but also somewhat British.

The national game here is cricket, and I wandered into the National Stadium this morning to watch a test match between Bermuda and the United States. The two flags whipped on the flagpole, the Bermudan flag being a bright red with the Union Jack in the top left-hand corner and their coat of arms in the middle. The very sparse crowd watched the players, all in white of course, running about in the heat, while the sound of leather on willow clattered across the ground.

Bermuda is a tropical paradise, and most of the American tourists who visit here on the big white cruise ships must find it curiously British, with the different accents, the cricket and the relaxed way of life. For the British, arriving from London, it must appear more American, with the crowds of American tourists about them, the souvenir shops, the US dollar currency, the television channels and the American food in the supermarkets and restaurants.

Bermuda is synonymous, of course, with 'The Bermuda Triangle', that mysterious legend of disappearing planes and ships. In fact, the Bermuda Triangle is a vast area of ocean between Bermuda in the northeast, to Florida in the west, and to Puerto Rico in the south. In this triangle, which is also known as 'The Devil's Triangle', it is thought that hundreds of ships and planes have disappeared without a trace. The most prominent of these disappearances was in 1945 when five US Navy planes flew from Florida on a routine mission, and all disappeared, as did the search plane that went after them. Over the years, however, most people regard the underlying cause for these disappearances as a combination of human error and misjudgement in a vast area where weather fluctuations are significantly high.

The most distinctive part of Bermuda, for me, has been the prevalence of pink. The island's beaches are renowned for their pink-tinged sand, which obtain their colouring from the crushed shells of a tiny marine invertebrate called a foraminifer. Reflecting their pride in their pink beaches, the locals seem to have embarked on an elaborate marketing campaign, making everything else pink in the process. Many of the public buildings and houses are painted pink, as is the main hotel on the island, The Hamilton Princess. Nature seems to have taken it upon itself to make other things pink as well – the Bermudan flamingos are bright pink, almost orange; the scarlet ibis is a beautiful pink colour and the undersides of the dolphins at the marine pools are a curious shade of pink. The charity organisation here is known as 'The Pink Ladies', the public buses are all pink, and many of the trees and flowers on the island are pink – oleander, hibiscus and hydrangea.

But the one item of pink that really stands out is the businessman's Bermuda-style short pants, worn with long black socks, smart black shoes and a jacket and tie.

It's what they wear here in downtown Hamilton. In the oppressive heat that is midsummer in Bermuda, it is entirely sensible.

CHAPTER THIRTY-THREE

The Rare Bermudan Sea Otter

Shelly Bay Beach, Bermuda
July 12th — 32°19'58.21"N, 64°44'22.15"W

Searching for a platypus on the island of Tasmania many years ago, Robbo and I found a stream at the bottom of the Roschecombe Vineyards, where the little creature was known to live. We staked it out for several hours, and finally, our patience paid off. From underneath a broken tree trunk, the platypus swam quickly across the water and disappeared, but not before we had captured the moment on film. We were jubilant and added it to our 'scalps' of Tasmanian wildlife. Two days later, on the return plane to Sydney, I was browsing through a book on Tasmania's native animals when I came across the creature. 'Water Rat,' the caption read. That is what we had seen, not a platypus!

Last night, Caroline, Craig and I enjoyed a sundowner near the beautiful Shelly Bay Beach, looking out over the quiet waters as the sun set over a far distant America. A movement in the water attracted our attention, and we squinted to make out what it was. It was not a fish. It was not a bird. It was not a seal, or a dolphin, or a turtle. It disappeared every now and then beneath the surface, only to reappear a few metres further on, casually splashing about on top of the water.

'It looks like an otter,' I said, and Caroline and Craig nodded sagely. An otter it must be. 'And on my first night here,' I thought, very pleased with myself.

Whenever I travel to faraway places, it is the wildlife that fascinates me the most, I think. I remember being enchanted in Greenland by the huskies and the snow buntings – delightful little black and white birds that have adapted so well to their harsh surroundings. I was also drawn to the promise of polar bears, arctic foxes and fatefully, seals. In Iceland, of course, I was introduced to the puffins, and in Rum it was the turn of the Rum ponies, the Highland cattle, the feral goats and the red deer to grab my fascination. In Lapland, I had aspirations of finding bears and moose, elk and wolverines and beavers, but I had to be satisfied with reindeers and squirrels and one lonely arctic hare.

Arriving in Bermuda, I immediately made inquiries as to what native wildlife I might find and was a bit disappointed to find that these were limited to green turtles and an impressive array of bird- and sea-life.

The coral reefs surrounding Bermuda are the northernmost coral reefs in the Atlantic and owe their existence to the warm ocean currents of the Gulf Stream. There are over four hundred different types of fish around Bermuda, and a lazy afternoon snorkel along the coast turned into a veritable smorgasbord of fish life. It was great to find beautiful pufferfish, blue angelfish, little yellow sergeant majors, blue puddingwifes, black-tailed breams and the branch impersonating trumpet fish.

This morning, Craig and I visited the Bermuda Aquarium, Museum & Zoo, the pre-eminent institution on the flora and fauna of the islands, and I resolved to solve the mystery of our rare find of the Bermudan sea otter.

'Are you the right person to speak to about rare sightings of animals?' I asked a rather healthy looking, large woman at the front desk, dressed in an impressive blue uniform. Beside her sat a younger man, in a matching outfit. He was playing chess on a computer and looked bored.

'We spotted something rather unusual down at Shelly Beach,' I began, and the woman began to nod slowly at me.

'It was an otter,' blurted Craig behind me, ruining my careful suspense.

'An otter?' said the woman, frowning. Beside her, the chess game ended suddenly as a pair of big round eyes stared at us. 'We don't have otters in Bermuda,' said the woman.

'It was an otter,' said Craig, with the authority of one who has lived in Bermuda for three whole months and knows what he saw.

'Well,' I said, describing what we saw, 'it wasn't a seal, or a turtle, or a fish, or a bird.'

'How about a dog?' asked the chessman, helpfully. Craig did not take this well.

'It was NOT a dog,' said Craig.

'I had better look into this,' said the woman, writing on a piece of paper. 'Can you explain exactly where you saw it?' she said to us and wrote down Craig's directions.

'Sometimes,' she said, 'we do have strange animals that make an appearance from time to time.'

I tried to comprehend what she had just said. The nearest land was a thousand kilometres away.

'I will send someone over right away to check it out,' she said. In Bermuda, it doesn't take much to create a stir!

As we left them, something occurred to her, and she called us back.

'You don't think it could perhaps have been a water rat?' she said, frowning again.

'A water rat?' I repeated as a cold feeling washed over me, an embarrassing memory from long ago.

'Yes,' she said, 'we do have water rats in Bermuda.'

'Perhaps,' I thought to myself as we headed for the parking lot and the scooter ride home, 'perhaps it is time for me to abandon this frolic with natural history and let the people who know what they're doing get on with it!'

CHAPTER THIRTY-FOUR

The Statue Who Gave Me a Ride

Barnes Corner, Hamilton, Bermuda
July 13th — 32°17'34.68"N, 64°46'11.21"W

It may be because this nation has never been invaded, or that courtesy is hammered into them as they grow up, or maybe it is the simplicity of island life, but the people of Bermuda are exceedingly friendly. Walk down the street, or go into a shop, and you'll be met with a 'Good morning, how are you?' or if not words, then at least a smile. It's a way of life here, a way of relating to one another.

On the local bus yesterday afternoon, the bus driver was a large black woman of about fifty, with the braids in her hair tight against her scalp and great clumps of gold bangles around her wrist. She talked at the top of her voice about this or that, and quite often other locals in the bus would shout something back at her, even though they appeared to not know each other. As each person got off the bus at their particular stop, in an unhurried way, she'd open the door, look them in the eye, and say, 'You have a nice afternoon now, you hear'.

My niece Caroline works at the local hospital here and relates how each morning she must greet each person in her department. Now, this is all fine and could be considered normal. Unfortunately for her, the bathrooms are at the far side of the department and to go to the loo she needs to speak to everyone twice more, once on the way there and the other on the way back. Not to do so is considered abnormal, rude even.

When Bermudans are in their motorcars or on their scooters, greeting people with a 'Hello' or a 'Hi, How you all doin?' is obviously not possible, but this is why motor manufacturers put hooters onto cars and scooters, of course. Walk along any Bermudan street, and you will at first be alarmed at the torrent of toots that come from all directions. There are only sixty thousand people on the island of Bermuda, and it's odds on that you will know at least one in three people you see. So they hoot, and they toot, and they honk their way around the island – greeting, greeting, greeting. The buses do it, the taxis do it, the ferries do it, the cars do it, and the scooters do it. Everyone does it. It's the way things are done.

A little over twenty years ago, one particular man would walk to the bus station where he worked, and on his way, he would greet everyone he met with a 'Good morning, how are you?' or even a 'God bless you this lovely morning'. Then one morning something made him wander over to an island in the middle of the road, and wave to all the passing cars. He stood there with outstretched arms and called to the cars. 'Good morning to you,' he would call. 'God bless you all.'

He noticed the surprised looks on the faces of the motorists, and a few people even waved back. The next morning on his way to work, he stopped there again, and some of the people who had seen him the morning before waved to him this time, perhaps even smiled. The next day he got up even earlier.

Twenty years later he is still there, every weekday morning from six until ten, standing on his little island, waving. This morning I decided to visit Mister Johnny Barnes, of Crow Lane roundabout.

Caroline gave me a ride on the back of her scooter which she parked carefully some way down the road, and the two of us made our way towards the traffic circle. From a distance, we could hear the tooting, and as we neared, could make out the little figure of Johnny Barnes, wearing long blue trousers and a faded long sleeve shirt in the print of an island scene. His black face peeked out beneath a broad white hat and was shrouded by a white beard of magnificent proportions. Near to him, hanging on the yield sign, was a red bag, and an umbrella lay against the pole. On either side of him, the traffic came and went, hooting all the time. His body was a little bent, and he made quite a sight, extending his arms out towards the cars in greeting, a big smile emanating from his small face.

He saw us and smiled, motioning for us to join him on his little island. We scampered between the traffic and shook hands with Johnny. His grip was strong, as was his gaze. He greeted us with a 'How are you both?' and we asked if we could take a photograph. Each of us stood beside him in turn for our photo, as the cars continued to rush by – hooting, hooting, hooting.

He asked where we were from, and when Caroline explained that she lived here and that I was visiting from South Africa, Johnny looked disappointed.

'You two look like lovers,' he said, smiling out from under his beard. We laughed. 'Oh, no,' said Caroline, 'he's my uncle!'

'Oh, I'll marry you then,' laughed Johnny.

Over the past twenty years, Johnny Barnes has become a Bermudan legend, and people come from far and wide to see him. He is an institution, a permanent fixture.

'What made you stand out here that first morning?' I asked Johnny. His back was to the traffic now, and we had his full attention.

He looked us over before answering. 'When the Good Lord says you to do something,' said Johnny, 'you'd best obey Him.'

To support himself, Johnny sells postcards and posters of himself to passers-by. We bought a few to send home and, emboldened by all this personal attention from him, we pushed a few more questions his way.

'You young people,' he said, 'you have a long life ahead of you. Don't mess it up. So many people mess it up.' He looked at us sternly. 'You only have one chance. Don't mess it up now.'

He is over eighty now, he told us and used to stand here for an hour or so each morning for three or four years before he retired from his regular job in the late 1980's. Since then he's been here every weekday, rain or shine, for four hours each morning.

When the Queen visited Bermuda, one of her scheduled stops was at Crow Lane roundabout, at Barnes' Corner, as it had become known.

"Hello, my darling', I called to her,' said Johnny, "I love you."

'And what did she say?' asked Caroline.

His eyes gleamed. 'She said, 'Hello, Johnny, I love you too."

'She only came at four in the afternoon, so I had to come here especially just to wave to her,' he laughed.

As we were leaving, he asked if I'd be travelling soon, and made us all hold hands and close our eyes, three people forming a little prayer circle on a busy roundabout in the morning traffic.

He prayed. 'Our loving heavenly father (HOOT HOOT), you have placed us (TOOT) on God's green earth (TOOT TOOT) to do your will in the world. (HOOT) Thank you for bringing us (HOOT HOOT) safely here today, and we pray your blessings (TOOT TOOT) for safe travel for this traveller.'

He hugged us each goodbye, and we made our way through the traffic to the distant pavement. Caroline headed off for the hospital on her scooter, and I wandered up the street, shaking my head and marvelling at how fate so often waits till late in someone's life before giving them the chance to make their greatest impact.

A little further up the road, I came across a life-size bronze statue of Mister Johnny Barnes, arms outstretched in his familiar pose. At the base of the statue was inscribed the words, 'Spirit of Bermuda', that great spirit of friendship that Johnny embodies so well. Nicknames he has been called in the past include 'Mr. Feelgood' and 'The Happy Man'. I am sure that when Johnny passes on one day to that great roundabout in the sky, his statue will be moved to where he stands now. After some time spent taking photographs, I wandered down to the bus stop to wait for the bus to town where I planned to spend the rest of the morning. Not two minutes later, I spotted Johnny hobbling past on the other side of the road, carrying his red bag and umbrella.

He called to me. 'What you doing over there?', and when I answered, he waved me across to him. 'I'll give you a ride,' he said. 'Come with me. I'll give you a ride.'

I crossed the road and walked with him towards his car. I asked him about the statue.

'They said to me, 'We're going to build a statue of you when you die one day.' I said to them, 'Don't do it when I die. Do it now.'' He paused, remembering something. 'Got very tired standing for that statue, I did.'

Johnny stopped on the pavement beside me and looked up at me. 'When I die it's too late to appreciate it. A man must appreciate things when he's alive,' he said.

We walked into a small parking lot and found his car, a dark-blue Mitsubishi, about five years old. A van pulled up alongside it, and a bearded man of about sixty called out, 'How are you today, Mr Barnes? How are you, brother?' Johnny waved to him as the van drove off.

Fascinated by this little old man, this Bermudan legend offering me a ride in his car, this octogenarian with his red tog bag and umbrella, I asked him lots of questions as he slowly prepared for departure, taking giant gulps of water from a canister on the back seat.

He was born in Bermuda in 1923, and apart from some time living in New Hampshire, spent all his life here in Bermuda. His wife, Belvina, and he have been married for over fifty years. They never had children. He used to work as a bus driver, and nowadays, apart from his duties at the roundabout, busies himself with his gardening and chasing away the feral chickens. 'I didn't tell my wife what I was doing, at first,' he chuckled, 'she thought I was having an affair!'

Our route as we drove took us directly past the statue, and I had the surreal experience of waving to a statue while sitting next to the man himself! I laughed as I waved, and Johnny gave a familiar 'TOOT' at the statue with the outstretched arms. We talked on as Johnny drove exceedingly slowly into town, cars passing us all the time.

As he stopped to let me out, I thanked him again, but he stopped me. 'You know,' he said, looking across at me, little man behind big steering wheel, his large brown hands crinkled with age, 'if every individual in this world could just do one thing to make another person happy, just one thing, imagine what a difference that would make.'

As I shook his hand one last time he looked me in the eye and said again, 'Just one thing'.

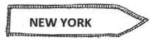

CHAPTER THIRTY-FIVE

The A-Train to Spanish Harlem

Lenox Jazz Lounge, Harlem, New York City
July 17th — 40°48'26.06"N, 73°56'43.45"W

'You bin bitin' the girls then?' he asked me, straight off the bat, his eyebrows raised.

He was my cab driver, giving me a ride from Smith's Parish to Bermuda airport, about a twenty-minute drive. I try not to talk to cab drivers, but this one was quite forthright and insisted that I sat up front with him.

His name was Walli Mohammed and he was a native Bermudan, a black man in his mid-sixties. 'Walli', according to him, means friendship, and 'Mohammed' means praiseworthy.

'You bin bitin' the girls?' he said again, in the strange British West Indian accent, 'You bin going with the local girls here then?'

'Excuse me?' I said, not understanding the words or the context.

'You bin bitin' the girls then?' he said again, in the strange British West Indian accent. 'You bin going with the local girls here then?'

'Um, no,' I answered, my eyes boggling a little at his forthrightness. 'Just visiting friends,' I added.

'Ahh, shy are you?' said Walli, his head covered in greying stubble, his lips leathery and big. He gave a long, drawn-out hoot as he stopped suddenly for a pedestrian. He turned and looked me in the eyes.

'What you gotta do,' he said, intent on conveying wisdom, 'you just gotta say a coupla words to em, to get started, you know, and then you're away.' He laughed. 'Oh, you'll be bitin' em alright.'

It was when I said that I was going to New York that he really began to talk, and I heard the life story of Mr Walli Mohammed. He was formerly of the Royal Navy and the British Royal Artillery. He was also a former clarinet and saxophone player and perhaps most importantly, a jazz aficionado and expert on New York City.

'Oh man,' he said, remembering. 'Early sixties – man I knew 'em all – Johnny Coltrane, Ella Fitzgerald, Billie Holliday.'

As we pulled up at the airport and he helped me hoist my backpack onto my shoulders, we shook hands, and he said to me.

'Man, I wish I was comin' with you. Hell, I'd take you up on the A-train to Spanish Harlem, up to 125th Street on Eighth – that's where all the action is,' he said. I could see the regret in his eyes.

'We'd go on a Saturday – go where all the Spanish people – you know, the Cubans and the Puerto Ricans – where they all just hang out on the sidewalk.'

'That's where we'd go,' he said quietly, as our hands parted.

I'm not sure why I did it, why I went to Harlem today, Saturday night in New York. Perhaps it was for Walli, remembering that sad look in his eyes. Perhaps it was for the promise of jazz – the laid-back music that crosses generations. But mostly, I think, it was my adherence to chance, to fate. I've tried to do this whenever possible on this trip – keep my options open, my itinerary flexible so that when something interesting comes along, I can follow the trail. That's why I went to Rum. That's why I ended up in Norway, and why I went back to Santa. And that's why I went to Harlem.

Just in case you think I'm entirely carefree, I did make one side trip to make sure of my information. I found the largest music store I could find, and in their jazz section, I sought out the oldest African American person. He couldn't have been more helpful and reinforced my belief in what Walli had told me. He also recommended a club in Harlem called 'The Lenox Lounge' that was legendary in the jazz world.

Using the number two or three trains to reach Harlem would have been a lot easier, but I listened to Walli and took the A-train instead and found my way to 125th and 8th. There was a pawnshop on one corner, a fast-food restaurant on another and a lot of Hispanic and African American people hanging about everywhere. There was no sign of any jazz clubs there, so I wandered down 125th, which is also called Martin Luther King Jnr. Boulevard. It's an enjoyable walk – down pavements fringed with informal sellers, posters and T-shirts of Che Guevara, a

Martin Luther King speech blaring out from a TV set on the sidewalk, and stickers reading 'Buy Black'. At one point I was caught up in an informal group discussion of about thirty people about repressed memories of slavery, where I felt very out of place.

Walking a little further, past the famous Apollo Theatre, at the corner of Martin Luther King Jr. and Malcolm X Boulevards, I found it – The Lenox Lounge. Billie Holliday played there, as did John Coltrane and Miles Davis; Malcolm X used to hang out there, and it's been hosting jazz in Harlem since 1939.

I was early for the main show, featuring the Arlee Leonard Trio and sat in the bar for an hour or so, sitting at the bar counter and writing the first parts of this story – about Walli and the delight of chance.

Later, alone with my Jack Daniels and notebook, I sat with the small crowd in the lounge, a dark room with chairs and tables, red upholstery and mirrors, listening to the melodic sounds of Arlee Leonard. My feet tapped involuntarily as the jazz trio of drums, piano and bass guitar worked up a sweat with their soulful tunes.

In rare moments of silence, when the applause subsided and the band set up for their next song, the Saturday night street noises of Harlem drifted in, and I found myself watching the door, half hoping that Walli Mohammed might walk in, and take me back with him to those days long ago when John Coltrane and Louis Armstrong ruled the world.

  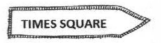

HARLEM

TIMES SQUARE

CHAPTER THIRTY-SIX

Next to Naked

Times Square, New York City
July 18th — 40°45'32.44"N, 73°59'04.10"W

'Could I have my photo taken with you?' I said sheepishly to the naked guy next to me.

This was Times Square, New York City, and I was standing on the centre island, surrounded by women and the tall buildings that look down on Seventh Avenue and Forty Second Street. The naked guy was actually 'The Naked Cowboy', a confident blonde Adonis from Texas, who stands in Times Square all year round. His fans just call him 'Naked'. He was clad in white underpants, cowboy boots (with spurs), a big Stetson hat and a guitar plastered over in red, white and blue stickers proclaiming 'The Naked Cowboy'.

I had heard of this strange dude and, after my experience with Mr Johnny Barnes, of Crow Lane Roundabout, I thought that the naked guy would make an interesting comparison.

I arrived a little before one today, but there was no sign of Naked, although Spiderman was making a brisk trade in the photography business. Just up the road I found a corner hot dog kiosk, and enjoyed an iconic New York hot dog, layered up with ketchup and barbecue Frito chips! Alerted by the distinctive shrieks of female voices, I returned to the scene to find that Spiderman had scattered and Naked had arrived. Standing about six foot five, he had quite a presence and added to it by tossing his long blonde hair about and strumming his guitar loudly, his voice screeching out the distinctive sound of country. He wore tight white briefs with *USA* handwritten in red ink on the one side and *Naked Cowboy* on his bum. His white Stetson hat had *Naked Cowboy* stencilled in, and the only other clothing he wore was a pair of white leather boots, with *TIPS* written on the boot leggings above them.

Women flocked from all directions to have their photo taken with him, their male companions hanging back undecided, or even retreating across the street in mild embarrassment. Putting my inhibitions behind me, I pressed forward in the line, listening to some of his favourite one-liners.

'Let's go, folks, step up and get your photo. No wasting time. Only one second with the king.'

The only other guy on the island with me, apart from the naked guy, was a big, African American fellow with a mouth of white teeth that he flashed constantly.

'Makes a thousand dollars a day,' he said to me, nodding his head towards Naked.

Naked was in his element, flirting with the women and smiling photogenically in a dozen different poses.

I reached the front of the line and found a friendly lady to take a photograph.

'Could I have my photo taken with you?' I said sheepishly to Naked.

He didn't bat an eyelid. 'Of course,' he said, taking charge. 'How about we stand back to back?'

So there we stood, Naked and I, leaning against each other, arms folded importantly out in front of us, grinning at the camera, the bright billboards of Times Square all around. With the photograph taken, I slipped a few notes into Naked's leather boots and delayed the women in the line a little longer.

'What made you stand out here the first day?' I asked, remembering asking Johnny Barnes the same question.

The Naked Cowboy didn't seem to mind the delay.

'I made myself stand out here,' he said, and I remembered Johnny Barnes saying, 'when the Good Lord says you to do something, you'd best obey Him.'

When Naked saw I was not satisfied with that answer, he went on in his broad Texan accent, 'Well, I reviewed my personal, my spiritual, my financial, my economic goals, and I decided what I had to do. I decided to dominate the world.'

He looked at me strangely, as if I might be a journalist.

'I've got a multi-million dollar business right here,' he said, 'I'm the third biggest tourist attraction in New York City, and by this time next year it will be a billion-dollar business.'

As if he wasn't sure I would believe him, he said to me as he shook my hand, 'You should check out my website – www.nakedcowboy.com.'

I left the centre island and wandered across to the Times Square information office where I checked out his website on their free internet service.

'I had a bare, empty apartment,' Naked was quoted as saying, 'with mirrors on every wall. I had a knife, a fork, a bed, a guitar and thirty-six pairs of underwear. I had an overwhelming fascination with being the centre of attention. What would you do?'

I walked out again onto Times Square and, from a distance, watched the throngs of women frolicking with Naked while behind them, in a giant advertisement for Gillette, a ten-storey high David Beckham stared down provocatively.

As I turned to leave, I wondered what Mister Johnny Barnes, standing on his roundabout in Crow Lane, Bermuda, would make of the Naked Cowboy standing on his island in Times Square.

'Into the Land of Pink'
A Bermudan businessman in typical dress
(his pants were bright pink)

'The Statue Who Gave Me a Ride'
Mister Johnny Barnes and Caroline at Crow Lane Roundabout,
and below, the statue of Mister Johnny Barnes

'Next to Naked'
The Naked Cowboy and Rich in
Times Square, New York

CHAPTER THIRTY-SEVEN

The Elf That Got Away

Nanaimo, Vancouver Island, Canada
July 20th — 49°10'33.91"N, 123°55'24.41"W

In faraway Lapland, where vast forests of pine trees hide under an enormous cloth of snow, the elves of Santa Claus work night and day, their small fingers busily crafting toys for the good children of this world. Force-fed with Mama Claus's porridge and resorting to stolen moments with special friends, their lives sometimes become intolerable, and some may resort to extraordinary measures. Typically, they reassign such elves to other duties, such as herding reindeer or mixing paint, but occasionally, once in a blue moon, one might escape.

An escaped elf needs to do everything in his power to remain escaped, for if caught, the consequences are too dire to be spoken of here. Escaped elves need to go far, far away – to the other end of the world...

On a street corner in Vancouver, Canada, on a chilly Tuesday evening in July, quite near to a bus stop, stood just such an elf.

He was old, perhaps around seventy, but he still had that distinctive elvish build – short and slight – and he had long, shaggy white hair, just a little like Santa's. His hair stuck out in all directions from underneath his bright green hat and hung in clumps of white on his bright green shirt. The skin on his face was leathery and looked to be somewhat oversupplied. The end of his nose was quite red, a bit like Rudolph, and so were his lips, in stark contrast to the bright green of his floppy hat. He wore metal-rimmed glasses crudely fixed with a piece of bent wire on the edge of the frame. He had that weathered look about him, and his fingernails were filled with dirt.

On his feet, he wore an old pair of white sneakers that gave the impression that he walked a lot. Like from Lapland, for instance.

But of all the impressionable accessories that the old elf wore, it was the dozens of little wooden badges pinned onto his shirt and hat, which invited the most questions.

Each badge had a different slogan burned into a circle of pine.

151

Make Love Not War, read one. *Be Fossil Fuel Obscene*, read another. *Vote for a Future – Go Green*, read a third.

Not far from the old green elf, standing at the bus stop waiting for bus 275 to Horseshoe Bay Ferry Terminal, was a girl in her mid-twenties, surrounded by luggage. She was blonde and pretty and didn't believe in Santa Claus or elves. She looked like she had been on a long journey and just wanted to get to where she was going. She had seen the old green elf – everybody had – but she had tried to avoid making eye contact. As she saw him walking directly towards her, she looked down at her shoes, counting to two.

'Where you from? You got lots of bags,' said the elf, by way of introduction, not looking for an answer.

The girl tried to avoid him and gave short answers, but soon it was clear that he had all the time in the world. When her bus arrived, he said, 'Oh good, that's my bus too,' and followed her onto the bus. She purposefully sat in an empty seat next to a lady with a baby so that the elf couldn't sit next to her and settled comfortably back, listening to music through her earphones.

At the first stop, the lady with the baby got off the bus, and the elf quickly changed seats and pointed at the girl's earphones, making it clear that he wanted to talk to her. She still didn't know he was an elf; she just thought he was weird.

Over the next few minutes, the girl and the elf began to learn a little about one another. He heard that she was from South Africa and was travelling to Vancouver Island to meet her tall, dark and handsome boyfriend, after a long time apart. She heard that the elf had been attending a folk festival in Vancouver and lived on Vancouver Island, where he repaired electric motorbikes when he wasn't saving the world. He didn't mention Santa or his epic escape from Lapland.

His name was Kim. Her name was Jacky.

Jacky got off the bus first and managed to evade the elf as she boarded the ferry to Vancouver Island, but he tracked her down again and sat beside her, continuing the conversation as if nothing had happened.

The topic of discussion changed to all the wooden badges stuck to his hat and shirt. Jacky looked them over carefully – some of them were difficult to decipher:

Keep Canada Clean. Let's not be the Tail of the U.S. War Dog Obscene
Proud Canadians don't pay in blood money for US imperialism
Say No to the No-Paper Trail
Electric Bikes for Pedal Power Plus
Imperialism, Invasion, Poverty and Corruption Beget Terrorism
In a moment of light-headedness, she suggested a new one to him.
Strip Mining Prevents Forest Fires. He liked it. He wished he could set
fire to Lapland.

After a while, Jacky went in search of the cafeteria, buying a
hamburger and chips and sitting quietly at a table by the window.

She wanted to be alone. She was exhausted.

Two minutes later, Kim, the ageing green elf, was there at her side
again, clutching a cup of coffee.

'They give free refills, you know,' he said proudly.

'I think I'm going slightly mad,' said Jacky to herself as she ate her
hamburger, the elf man rambling on monotonously beside her.

As she ate the last of her hamburger, he pointed to her fries and
said, 'Are you not going to eat that?'

Resignedly, she passed him the plate, and as the elf ate her fries and
drank his free refill of coffee, she gazed longingly at the approaching
land. By now she had given up on the conversation for Kim's monologue
was uninterruptible, each sentence fading into another.

After the food, he scribbled notes of 'Vancouver Island Must Sees'
on a free tourist brochure for her, and sold her the wooden badge that
said *Make Love, Not War.*

When the ferry docked, they finally went their own ways – Jacky to
reunite with Rich, her long-lost writer boyfriend, and Kim, the old,
green elf, to do whatever it is that ageing escaped elves living out their
lives in distant lands happen to do.

As Jacky turned to wave goodbye to her little green man, she spied a
small wooden badge that she hadn't seen before.

Screw Santa, it said, but she couldn't be sure.

CHAPTER THIRTY-EIGHT

The Great International World Championship of Bathtub Racing

Salt Spring Island, Vancouver, Canada
July 23rd — 48°52'53.50"N, 123°34'21.36"W

Waiting for the car ferry to Salt Spring Island to arrive, Jacky and I noticed the unusual sight of a man in a bathtub. He was not in a house; he was not in a room. He was, in fact, in a floating bathtub on the water. He wore a crash helmet and a life jacket, and his little bathtub had an engine on the back. It also had a specially fitted sharply pointed front and sides to enable it to skim through the water and was brightly painted with a sign proclaiming it as *The Salt Springs Island Police Bathtub*. It was a bizarre sight.

We made our way down to the water and joined a rather portly man gazing out at the bathtub. His name, we would discover, was John.

'It's a gnarly venture,' said John, 'a real gnarly venture.'

'What is?' Jacky asked.

'Bathtub racing,' said John, looking a little surprised at us, and still gazing out at the bathtub. 'He'd better watch out, that one,' he said, pointing out onto the water with his chin, 'once he gets out onto the chuck, it gets real gnarly out there.'

'Gnarly?' I asked.

'Yeah, gnarly,' said John, staring.

The Great International World Championship Bathtub Race, as it is known, takes place this coming Sunday in Nanaimo, an annual event that has been running since 1967. It forms part of the Nanaimo Marine Festival that starts the week before with the Silliest Boat Race, another maniacal event that results in most participants sinking shortly after the start.

This year's bathtub race has seventy competitors and after a standing start at Nanaimo harbour, circles Entrance Island and Winchelsea Island before finishing in Departure Bay, where the winner has to run up the beach and ring a brass bell.

'It's thirty-two miles, you know,' said John, 'and it's hard – it's hard on the body,' he added, speaking from experience it seemed.

'It really beats you up – your kidneys, your sides – they're shot by the end of it. You've got to be young to do this. I once had to go out and rescue a buddy of mine – he was all beat up.'

Jacky and I were now reunited after two months away and looking forward to catching up on a seven-day cruise up to Alaska. We've been dating for around two years, and even though we're both from the same town in South Africa, we met at a wedding in New Zealand. We've never seemed to notice our fourteen year age gap (I'm the older one!) and everything is a lot more fun when Jacky is around – which is a good sign! She is a geologist by training, and when we met, was the only woman among ten thousand miners working underground at a platinum mine in South Africa. My visits to the mine single quarters hostel had to be clandestine and carefully arranged!

We were visiting with old friends on Vancouver Island. We borrowed their car and were exploring the surrounding islands near to Nanaimo when we came across John and his interesting views on bathtub racing.

'The problem with the bathtub,' said John, 'is that out on the chuck, when you're racing, the waves are big, and when they come into the boat, you've got to bail like anything.'

'Can't you just use the plug?' I asked, but John didn't get my joke.

After exhausting the tedious route of attracting industry or tourism to their small towns, it's almost as if the marketing people turn to the use of the extraordinary. So far I've found Wife-Carrying, Whistling, Phone Throwing, Mosquito Killing, Ice Swimming, Bog Snorkelling and the World's Best Liar. Now it's Bathtub Racing. Nanaimo, on Vancouver Island, brands itself 'the bathtub racing capital of the world'.

After a little while, the bathtub boat came into the shore for some adjustments to their tub, and we chatted with the driver and a friend who was helping him fine tune his bathtub. They were both local policemen. I asked him about his protective gear.

'You've gotta get padding – shin pads, knee pads, helmet – I need to put something under my arm here, where I hang on to the bathtub with my elbow,' said the bathtub racer.

'So are you a serious competitor?' I asked, remembering the Estonian Finnish rivalry in the Wife-Carrying.

'Yeah, pretty serious,' he said, his wetsuit rolled down to his waist now, 'the Aussies usually win though,' he added, 'they take it real serious.'

John, Jacky and I watched as the bathtub racer kitted up again, and headed out past the incoming ferry, the bathtub's little engine screaming.

'It's a gnarly thing, bathtub racing,' said John, 'a real gnarly thing.'

I would have liked to stay a few more days and watch the spectacle of the bathtub racing, but we had our own bathtub awaiting us. It was aboard the Royal Caribbean cruise liner, *The Vision of the Seas*, by far the fanciest vehicle of travel that I have used these past months! In figuring out the best way to reach Alaska, Jacky worked out that an inside cabin on a cruise ship can be booked for not much more than the combined cost of buses, ferries and stopovers, or flights, all the way to Anchorage. An inside cabin, if you haven't guessed it, means you don't have any windows, and you have to change your TV channel to number nine to see the view! However, considering there is so much to do on the ship, and see from the deck, you probably shouldn't be spending much time in your cabin anyway! So we'll be in comparative luxury for the next week, cruising up through the renowned Canadian Maritimes and Inside Passage, all the way from Vancouver to Anchorage, with stops at Ketchikan, Skagway, Juneau, Icy Straits and Hubbard Glacier.

Our first day aboard the cruise was full of surprises for us, and the staff, as we weren't well prepared or briefed on the right procedures. Our luggage was taken from us before we boarded, and would be delivered separately to our room. We were quite excited to get to our room, in more ways than one, and forgot entirely about our luggage, until the young delivery guy barged in without even a knock...

The passengers were all meant to be at a captain's briefing, or something – anywhere except in their rooms.

Much later, having taken in the sights from the top deck, we returned to our room, where the turn-down service had neatly tidied everything, and arranged our towels on the bed in the shape of two bears. Our bears, however, had been placed in a very compromising position...

There were more surprises at dinner, for we'd packed for a camping trip, not formal dining. We did our best, with a Hawaiian garland round Jacky's neck, and a faded denim jacket for me. As we neared our allocated table, my feet started backpedalling on their own accord. It was a table for twelve, and there were five elderly couples waiting to see who would join them for dinners every night this week. Retreating out of the dining hall, I slipped the maître d' a rather large banknote, and he arranged a private table for two at the back, next to the kitchen door. Much like our cabin, it had no view whatsoever. After two months apart, Jacky and I didn't feel like sharing each other with anybody else, and we had the best view we could want!

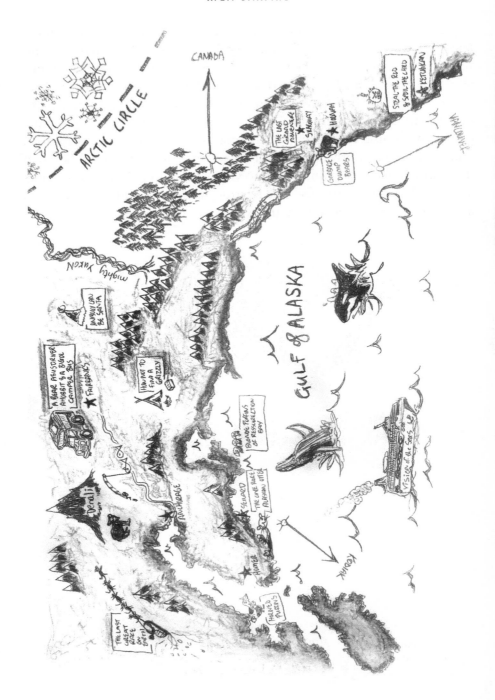

CHAPTER THIRTY-NINE

Steal the Rod and Spoil the Child

Ketchikan, Alaska
July 25th — 55°20'30.48"N, 131°38'46.36"W

I have been a little obsessed with finding whales on this cruise. Orcas and humpback whales are often seen along this route, so I have already spent a lot of time on the top deck, looking through binoculars and trying to find a crew member knowledgeable enough to know more than I do. Their mission, however, was with a different sort of whale.

With upwards of five different meals available per day on the cruise ship, their typical client, I soon found out, was not the whale-seeking pretend zoologist such as me, but someone entirely different. And the result of this was that, instead of finding orcas and humpbacks, we began finding other sorts of whales.

The first of these was the *buffet whale*, an oval-shaped whale with extended elbows, and an impressive ability to carry multiple plates at the same time. We usually found them at the tables closest to the food. We also identified *lounge whales*, who dominated the top deck loungers and had the food brought to them throughout the day. The easiest whales to find were immediately next to the swimming pool and were, of course, the *beached whales*. The *cocktail hour whales* might actually have been *buffet* or *lounge whales* in disguise, but they altered their appearance in the late afternoon and dominated the evening cocktail functions, showing enormous dexterity in grasping multiple snacks at the same time as a very large cocktail. However, our prize find, after midnight last night, was the nocturnal *midnight feast whale*, who clearly didn't get enough food during the day, and reappeared around midnight for the pizza and hot dogs that were mysteriously served at this late hour! Our search for the more regular whales continued, but in the meantime, we were being fully entertained.

This morning, on the tour order form aboard our cruise ship, one of the daily tours was advertised as follows:

Ketchikan Sportfishing – Fish in the 'Salmon Capital of the World' with well-equipped fishing boats designed to maximise your chances.

That sounded amazing, but also beyond both our budget and the way we wanted to experience the world, so we set off to explore on our own and hopefully, do some fishing at the same time.

The town of Ketchikan is the first stop for many of the cruise liners on their way north through the Inside Passage. It lies at the bottom of Alaska, some fifty miles from the Canadian border and is a pretty town set against the backdrop of mountains and forests of spruce trees. Ketchikan Creek is a windy stream that ends in the harbour and from there backs its way up the mountain through many gushing rapids alternating with broad, tranquil bends. The bridges provide perfect vantage points for watching the spectacle of salmon jumping.

The story of salmon is as much a part of Alaska's history as is gold and oil, and so much of life here revolves around the life cycle of the salmon. It's a fantastic story. Hatched in their millions from eggs laid in the gravel of mountain streams, they spend their first year or so trying to survive and gaining size in the place they were born. Then their body clock kicks in, and they begin to adapt to being able to live in seawater. They leave their little mountain stream and make their way down the river and out into the ocean. Four or five years later, if they survive the ocean challenges, they make their way home to the same little stream, climbing rapids and impossible looking waterfalls to get there.

Once there, the females lay their eggs, and the males fertilise them and then, exhausted by their strenuous efforts, they begin to die, provoking a feeding frenzy for the bears and birds of Alaska.

Salmon hatcheries have piggybacked the miracle of salmon, and the Ketchikan Deer Mountain Hatchery is a perfect example of man and nature in an unusual combination. They milk the eggs of the salmon, ensure they are fertilised, and then rear the young salmon, or fingerlings, in giant tanks where they are protected from predators and given a hugely increased chance at life. At thirteen months, by which time they are known as smolts, they are released into Ketchikan Creek and make their way out into the ocean. After a few years at sea, they return and at the point where the creek runs past the hatchery, netted barricades force the salmon to 'climb' a fish ladder (concrete pools set at different levels) and effectively catch themselves. Here the eggs are taken from the females, and their flesh becomes the famous Alaskan salmon that they serve up nightly on our cruise boat!

Jacky and I enjoyed our ramble through the little town and our visit to the hatchery, but it was our walk along Ketchikan Creek that was the most exciting. At a bend in the creek, we spotted the dark bodies of hundreds of king salmon, just holding themselves up against the current, motionless, as if storing up the energy to tackle the next set of rapids. We watched the big salmon climb the fish ladder into the hatchery, using their powerful tails to propel themselves through the waterfall and up into the pool above. We followed the creek all the way to the harbour, passing the old wooden buildings commemorating the days when this stretch of river was a place of ill repute, a haven for ladies of negotiable affection.

From the bridge we watched and chatted with the local fishermen who were trying to snare the incoming salmon with their colourful lures. They were not very successful at fishing, but their stories told us of a town desperately trying to survive.

Todd, one of the Ketchikan locals, a young guy with long blonde hair poking out from under a beanie, told us,

'There used to be good money in logging – not anymore though,' he said, his eyes following his line beneath the bridge, 'these days it's just tourism.'

After a little while, and with no sign of fish, Jacky nudged me and pointed to a small boy fishing from a nearby jetty.

'Let's go there,' she said.

He was about ten years old, a thin boy with a dark complexion and close cut hair.

'I'm Jordan,' he told us when we asked.

He was using a light rod, and his lackadaisical cast out into the channel told of long summers fishing here in the harbour.

I could see the look in Jacky's eyes. She really wanted to use that rod.

'Where are your parents?' she asked, trying to find an angle.

'Oh, they just hang out at home,' he said casually, jerking the rod rapidly back and forth, 'you know – as all parents do,' he added.

Further conversation revealed that his mom was in a wheelchair and his dad worked for a carpet cleaning company. After watching him fish a while longer we realised he wasn't fishing – he was fly-hooking. There were so many salmon in the river he was dragging the hook through the water as fast as possible, hoping to snag one. Pretty soon, he did.

161

The rod bent double as he began to reel it in.

Jacky stepped nearer to the small boy.

'Do you mind if I reel it in?' she asked, so nicely.

He seemed happy to let her have a turn, and for the next ten minutes she fought the fish, the little rod bent double, the people on the bridge watching the scene. When the beautiful fish was right below us, it made a final lunge for freedom and snapped the line.

The small boy shrugged as Jacky handed him back his rod. In a few minutes, he was trawling for fish again.

We gave Jordan a few dollars and thanked him before wandering off into town; Jacky still flushed with the excitement of the chase.

She was quite pleased with the fight with the fish too.

Back on the cruise ship this evening, we again avoided the crew members responsible for servicing our room, and found their little message to us - two elephants with unspeakable trunks.

Our busy day on land had meant we'd missed out on lots of ship activities such as gentle touch teeth whitening, jackpot bingo, brainteaser trivia, adult ping pong, margarita madness at the schooner bar, the 'Love and Marriage' game show, and for the whales, the 'Eat More to Weigh Less' seminar.

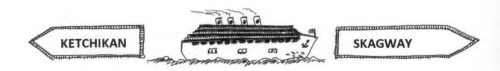

CHAPTER FORTY

The Last Grand Adventure the World Will Ever Have

Skagway, Alaska
July 26th — 59°27'13.65"N, 135°19'06.10"W

Ken Clineman, Park Ranger Extraordinaire, stood over us, his eyes ablaze with enthusiasm, with passion.

'When you come to Alaska and see the great mountains, the rivers, the deep valleys – it makes you realise you are part of the ecosystem, it puts your life into perspective,' he said.

You can always tell a great teacher by looking into their eyes. Their love of subject is infectious; it makes you want to follow, want to learn.

This afternoon we sat in the second row of the little auditorium of Skagway's Visitors Centre, waiting for the short film on the great gold rush of 1898 to begin. The back door burst open, and a tall, athletic man of about sixty walked purposefully to the front. He was dressed in the smartly ironed khaki uniform of a park ranger, with his greying hair tied behind his head in a long ponytail. If you add the uniform, the piercing look in his eyes and an impressive entrance, he was always someone who was going to get our attention.

Pointing to the large black and white photographs lining the walls, he placed his left foot on one of the seats in the empty front row and, looking down at us, said, 'After the film, I'd like you to look at the photos again. Look at the faces. Remember that each of the nameless faces had a name. Each had a family. Each had their own story.'

He paused, his eyes flitting across to the photographs, then back to us. 'I like to think of the gold rush of 1898 as a mosaic of personal stories.'

The Tlingit peoples who lived in Skagway in the late nineteenth century used the word 'Scagua' which means 'the place where the north wind blows'. A small bay at the very top of Canada's Inside Passage leads to Skagway, a tiny town dwarfed by huge mountains all around, their cliffs plunging down towards the ocean. At the start of 1897 it was a small settlement, three months later it was crammed with thirty thousand people, all of them on the great adventure of their lives.

On July 17, 1897, the headline of Seattle's Post-Intelligencer newspaper screamed out *Gold! Gold! Gold!* and reported that *68 Rich Men on the Steamer Portland* arrived in Seattle with *Stacks of Yellow Metal.*

The news spread across America, and a nation in the midst of a depression went crazy. Tens of thousands of hopefuls left their homes at the drop of a hat and found their way to Skagway and nearby Dyea, the closest landing points to the Klondike. Unfortunately for them, their journey had barely begun, for a treacherous journey of over six hundred miles still lay ahead. Each was required by the Canadian Mounties to bring one ton of supplies with them so that they did not starve during the long frozen winter. And each of them had to carry this weight over the big mountains.

The route from Skagway was known as 'White Pass' and from Dyea as 'Chilkoot Pass'. Rising three thousand feet high and with sheer cliffs and boulders interspersed with ice and snow, these passes became legendary in the long annals of gold mining.

A man might make as many as forty round trips over the difficult twenty-mile terrain, harassed all the way by Soapy Smith's thieving henchmen, and take as many as six weeks to haul his load to the top. From there it was a little easier to reach the shores of Lake Bennett where he had to build his own boat from the wood of Lake Bennett's trees. It is said that the sawing of the planks was such a cumbersome task that, 'two angels could not saw their first log without getting into a fight'. Once they had built their boat and the long winter waited out, they would load their ton of possessions aboard and brave the many rapids on the five hundred and fifty mile stretch to Dawson City and the Klondike goldfields.

When they eventually arrived, they found every possible site on the goldfields taken, and ended up working for others.

Over a hundred thousand people came to Skagway and Dyea, and fewer than thirty thousand made it to the Klondike. The others were dead or on the way south again. About four thousand prospectors found gold, but only a few hundred became rich.

But those that found no gold had still made it to the Klondike and would remember those days as the great adventure and high point in their lives.

A few years after the gold rush, in the year 1900, a railroad was built over the infamous White Pass, connecting Skagway with the Yukon and it was a feat of engineering recently honoured as one of thirty-six civil engineering marvels of the world. The hard labour of tens of thousands of men overcame geography in creating 'the railway built of gold'.

Jacky and I took the White Pass & Yukon Railway today on what is billed as 'the scenic railway of the world'. It was a spectacular twenty-mile trip to the summit of White Pass, a narrow gauge railway that hugs the sheer cliffs, crosses wooden bridges and bores through tunnels. Along the way, we passed Gold Rush Cemetery, where Soapy Smith was buried, Bridal Veil Falls, Black Cross Rock, Dead Horse Gulch, Inspiration Point and at many places, the same paths used by those famous men of 1898.

Sobered by the thought of the toils of these brave men, and in awe at the majesty of the spectacular scenery, we sought out the Skagway Visitors Centre to find out more about this historic place.

That's when we ran into Ken Clineman, Park Ranger Extraordinaire. After the film we sought him out, eager to find out the source of his great passion.

He greeted us warmly and was very happy to tell us about his life. He and his wife live in Florida but are out here during the summer, living ten miles up the valley 'where we have bears in our backyard sometimes'. This is the second year that they have come to Skagway and it is clear from his expressions that he has fallen deeply in love with the land and its history.

Back in Florida, he is retired, although he spends a lot of his time doing environmental education work. He has a reverence for those old gold miners that shines through him.

'Look at the photos,' he'd said to us earlier in the auditorium, 'look at their faces, and remember that they could be you or me.'

When we'd commented about how much he seems to enjoy his job, he responded quickly, 'If it's not fun, it's not worth doing.'

As we left Ken Clineman and the little town of Skagway, filled with its tourist shops and museums, and still dwarfed by the mountains all

165

around, I thought back to all those adventurers arriving here, with gold in their veins. The Klondike Gold Rush of 1898 has been called *The Last Grand Adventure the World Will Ever Have*, and that might be right. They came to find gold, but instead, they found adventure.

After our day in Skagway with Ken Clineman and friends, we returned to feed at the buffet trough, and from our table near the kitchen door, the whale sightings were restricted entirely to the buffet variety. Again, we'd missed action on the ship during the day such as the late riser breakfast, the 'Search for Singles' get together, the 'Adventure Scavenger Hunt', the 'Cellulite Secrets' seminar and the 'Country & Western Hoe Down' (dang!).

In our room, our mysterious friend had been busy again – two swans necking across our pillows and lots of little red heart chocolates!

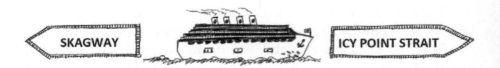

CHAPTER FORTY-ONE

In Search of the Garbage Dump Bears of Hoonah Island

Icy Point Strait, Hoonah Island, Alaska
July 28th — 58°06'35.12"N, 135°26'46.79"W

It is early evening off the Alaskan mainland, and I look out over a tranquil sea and a sky thick with overhanging cloud. Little islands dot the seascape in front of me, each of them entirely occupied by forests of tall spruce trees. Atop a few of them, a soft cloud of fog hangs motionless, waiting for a breeze.

As I scan the waters, I am expectant of drama, something that might emerge from below. Sitting on a comfortable chair in this same little lounge last night, my thousand yard stare was broken by the dramatic sight of a humpback whale breaching. Its entire body, except for its tail, was out of the water, a black shape against grey-blue, a great splash and a wake that went right across the bay. Again and again, it breached, again and again, I watched in awe, humbled by the majesty of it all.

The ship is now anchored in Alaska's Icy Straits, a long finger of sea renowned for freezing up in years past. The most significant island here, which is mostly uninhabited, is Hoonah Island, populated mainly by the Huna, the original Tlingit tribe that has lived in this area for centuries. It is, in fact, the largest Tlingit village in Alaska. Hoonah means 'village by the cliff', and is a beautiful place with everything that the word 'Alaska' brings to mind – mountains, forests, islands, mist, salmon and bears.

'Bears!' Now there's a word that gets my blood racing – perhaps even more than the word 'puffin'. Oh, to see a bear...

We were told there were bears on Hoonah Island, lots of them, and were so excited that we were the first off the boat this morning, catching the lifeboat connection to Icy Point, on the corner of Hoonah Island. There, we were distracted for a moment from our quest by an intriguing museum set in the old salmon packing sheds of the Hoonah Salmon Company where we learned first-hand the history of the salmon canneries in Alaska. In the main shed, the old production lines had been recreated with salmon, in all stages of canning, lying in the open – from whole fish to the finished cans.

They were all plastic but looked lifelike, and Jacky and I threw caution to the wind and, video in hand, pretended to be fish packers of old, throwing fish around and mishandling dangerous looking machinery. This was to the amazement of some of the tourists, who thought we were museum staff giving a demonstration.

A little later we met a Tlingit man called James who was standing out on Icy Point, tending a large fire. He was about sixty years old and wore a bright red jacket and a blue Vietnam Veterans' cap. He explained that this was a ceremonial fire and gave us woodchips of yellow cedar to throw into the flames. James said that the great totem poles were carved out of cedar and at the end of a ceremony called potlatch, all the guests would throw a few chips into the fire, for good luck and safe travel.

Many of the modern day Tlingit homes still have totem poles outside. The totem pole is not a religious pole but is used to tell a family story, honour someone who has died or be a celebration of good fortune.

Potlatch is a ceremony for raising a totem pole and guests come from far away for the festivities that might last many days. At Potlatch, it is customary for the host to provide all the food and, when he is celebrating good fortune, to give each guest an expensive gift. By giving everything away and starting over, he was honouring the community in which he had prospered. He also created the expectation that guests would return a gift of similar value in future.

In this most isolated of islands, a Tlingit Vietnam Veteran tended a ceremonial fire and shared with us the secrets of the potlatch.

On two different occasions, we watched Americans come up to James and thank him for his service in Vietnam. One man, of similar age to James, choked on his voice as he spoke of his brother who was shot down in Vietnam, and a lady, with white hair and a purple sweater, told James that she had a nephew serving in Iraq.

We asked James about the bears, and he confirmed that there were lots of them. 'We see them all the time,' he said, his one foot up on the big stones surrounding the fire. 'In the evening, when we're gone,' he said, 'they come right here.'

I looked right there and wished it were later.

We followed the walking path to a wooden information kiosk.

'Where can we see a bear?' I asked the young lady manning the kiosk.

'You're just too late,' she said, pointing to the nearby path, 'there was one right here two minutes ago.' We looked at the path, then back at her in amazement. 'Two minutes ago,' she said again, 'everyone scattered.'

'Will we still see it?' we asked, but she shook her head sadly. Then a look of pity came over her. 'Walking in this area is not allowed,' she said, 'but if you can get someone to take you to the garbage dump, you're sure to see them there.'

'The Garbage Dump Bears of Hoonah Island', I thought, 'now that would be a story!'

Finding locals to take us to the dump proved a difficult task, for they were banned from doing informal tours to the rubbish dump, as tourists are meant to pay top dollar for an 'organised' bear safari. For us, that was just too easy. The garbage dump route sounded more fun.

We took a local taxi for the short ride from Icy Point to Hoonah town, but the driver, a giant Tlingit man with selective hearing, seemed horrified at our proposal and refused outright. He did, however, drive us to his brother's cabin in the forest where he'd often seen bears. He found us the nest of a pair of bald eagles and we caught a glimpse of a chick, and at the edge of the forest, we found a beautiful young stag.

But no bears.

So it was that we found ourselves alone on the streets of Hoonah, seeking out an impressionable local who might lead us to bears.

The most likely candidate was a fat Tlingit girl with a severe acne problem. She would like to do it, she said, but she didn't have a car.

After a somewhat protracted search, we found our guide in a greasy fish and chip shop with plastic tables and very brown looking chip oil. She was a sizeable Tlingit woman of about forty and was dishing out great helpings of chips from the basket.

We explained our desperation to her.

'We've come all the way from South Africa,' Jacky said, 'and we are desperate to see the bears.' She looked us up and down for a long while, before giving us a small nod.

'I get off at two-thirty,' she said quickly, 'I could take you then.'

We thanked her profusely and promised to be back at the appointed time. With an hour or two to kill, we found a local pub that overlooked the little harbour and served beers and crab and played loud country music. Sort of my ideal place! Our crabs arrived on a large tray with a pair of pliers as our only utensil. When they ran out of crabs, they sent a few men out in a boat to empty the crab traps in the bay. Well-oiled and ready for the Garbage Dump Bears of Hoonah Island, we stumbled back along the Front Street of Hoonah to where Clarissa waited for us, alongside her beaten-up 1970's white Chrysler.

As we got to know each other a little better over coffee and ice-creams from a nearby store, Clarissa explained to us that if anyone stopped us, we're old friends who've come to visit her here on Hoonah Island. The story would be that Clarissa and I met years back when she was still working down the coast in Juneau. She used to be in the US Military in the southern United States, involved in radio and telephonic education, but now she's angry as they've lost her records and she can't be classified as a veteran. 'We're working on it,' they've told her.

Clarissa could be described as a voluptuous lady, with a round body and soft, beautiful eyes. Her black hair was long and hung down over her neck. Her face showed her age, and she had a black mole at the left-hand corner of her mouth, just below her lip. She wore royal blue homemade stretch pants and a black top that left a tasty circle of fat showing on her waistline.

She recently married a local man here in Hoonah, with whom she has been living for the past ten years.

'You just have to be sure,' Clarissa said of waiting such a long time to marry. She works as a part-time waitress and chef at the fish and chip shop, but her main job is packing fish at the local cannery.

We all climbed into her old Chrysler, which was an automatic with a stick shift attached to the steering column. Jacky sat up front with Clarissa, and I perched on the back seat along with the flotsam and jetsam of a long winter of casual littering.

We left Hoonah behind us as the big car motored up the hillside between forests of spruce trees and all of us feeling distinctly nervous whenever another car came from the opposite direction.

I thought the game was up when a utility vehicle screeched to a halt, and a scraggly-haired Tlingit man leapt out and strode across to us.

'It's alright,' said Clarissa, 'it's only my husband.'

Her husband stuck his face in the open rear window and stared at me, his unshaven face and missing teeth giving him the look of a wild man.

When Clarissa told him what we were up to, he shook his head to indicate we were most unwise.

'Best be quick about it,' he warned, and then he was off.

We continued for another few minutes before reaching the end of the road and found ourselves in a large quarry that led into a small ravine where piles of garbage smouldered. There was no sign of the Garbage Dump Bears of Hoonah Island.

'They must be fishing for salmon,' said Clarissa, 'I know a good place for us to look.'

The good place to look was twenty minutes in the opposite direction, and the drive took us through beautiful countryside, mostly forested or with thick tundra vegetation. It was a bridge set over a slow flowing stream that meandered in lazy half-moons, and the gravel banks were flat and perfect for bear fishing. To make conditions even better, the salmon were leaping out of the water, big salmon about two feet long.

But there were no bears.

On one side of the bridge, standing in the water, were two local fishermen, fishing poles in hand, and with rifles strapped to their backs.

Clarissa seemed even sadder than we were.

'No luck today, just no luck,' she said.

She drove us back to Icy Point slowly, all of us scanning the bush for our elusive bears. It was not our day.

But then again, thinking about it now, sitting here looking out over the beautiful calm sea and the forested small islands, maybe finding the Garbage Dump Bears of Hoonah Island was not what it was all about. We met and learned about the Tlingit peoples and their customs, we made a new friend, broke a few laws, ate crab and drank beer and went on an adventure of our own making.

But then again, thinking about it now, sitting here looking out over the beautiful calm sea and the small forested islands shrouded in mist, maybe finding the Garbage Dump Bears of Hoonah Island was not what it was all about. We met and learned about the Tlingit people and their customs, we made a new friend, broke a few laws, ate crabs and drank beer, listened to country music and went on an adventure of our own making.

Maybe it was our day after all.

Maybe, like the puffins of Vik, the bears of Alaska are waiting for us to earn our first sighting.

That way it will be all the more special.

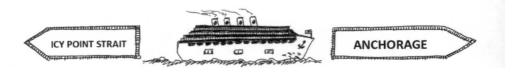

CHAPTER FORTY-TWO

The Last Great Race on Earth

Anchorage, Alaska
July 30th — 61°13'05.00"N, 149°51'01.00"W

'And no,' said the dark-haired woman standing in front of me, 'we don't cook our dogs!'

She looked to be in her mid-thirties, a friendly, jovial woman with brown, practical hair and a spring in her step. She was short, say about five feet two, with a round face and a sharpish sort of nose.

Her name was Erin McLarnon, and she and her husband have forty-seven dogs.

The sport of dog mushing evolved from the necessity of dog mushing, the only practical way to travel during the long Alaskan winters.

Many weeks ago now, in Greenland, I experienced the great thrill of riding on a husky sledge and living in a small Inuit village where huskies howled their hearts out each night. During those evenings, with the collective howls filling the air, I think I caught a sense of what it must be like to be a dog musher.

Erin and her husband live some eighty minutes by car from Anchorage, together with all their huskies. To support their enlarged family, they both keep regular jobs in Anchorage. It costs about a dollar a day to keep a husky.

We met Erin in Anchorage, one of the world's iconic place names, where she was giving an introductory lecture on dog mushing for the general public. She brought along one of her favourite dogs, Ruda, a beautiful black husky that barked loudly whenever he got excited, which was very often.

She was talking about all the things a dog musher needed to take along on a long distance mushing race – an arctic parka, an ice axe, snowshoes, food for the musher and the dogs, booties for the dog's feet, a cooker and so on – when she pre-empted the question about the cooking of dogs.

In the old days, the eating of dogs, by the musher and the dogs alike, was common practice, and a necessity. These days, however, it's a different story. At least to Erin.

We could see it in how she handled Ruda, how she talked about her dogs back home. 'We've got thirteen geriatrics now,' she said, 'they're between twelve and fifteen years old.'

The dogs, like those I lived amongst in Greenland, all live outside, although they do have some cover. 'We've also got two wimps that sleep in bed with us,' admitted Erin with a laugh.

Erin and her husband, Paul, like many other 'regular' people in Alaska – doctors, lawyers, fishermen, truckers – are dog mushers, a breed of people as unusual as the dogs they mush. They race against each other in mushing races that are followed here in Alaska as ardently as bicycle racing is in France. Indeed, the greatest race of them all, the Iditarod, is to Alaska what the Tour de France is to France.

The Iditarod is called 'The Last Great Race on Earth' and is an incredible race over some 1150 miles of the most inhospitable country, in the middle of the frozen Alaskan winter. They cross great mountain ranges, frozen rivers, dense forests, and miles of empty tundra and windswept coastline, to cover the distance from Anchorage in the southeast to Nome in the northwest, on the Bering Sea. They take between ten and seventeen days to complete the route, some choosing to travel by day, and others by night, although that said, there's not a lot of difference between the two! The teams of dogs can have anywhere between ten and seventeen dogs, and along the route, there are various checkpoints where veterinarians are on hand to check the dogs, and doctors to check up on the drivers.

The origins of the Iditarod, and its sister race, the Great Serum Race, which covers a shorter distance of 776 miles from Nenana to Nome, lie in a disaster which threatened to befall Nome in 1925 when many children contracted diphtheria and the only serum was in Anchorage. Teams of dog mushers ran relays all the way to Nome in an incredible six days, achieving immortality in the annals of Alaska, and enhancing the legend of the musher and his dogs.

'We don't actually use the word 'mush' on the sledge,' said Erin, 'believe me – the dogs need no help in getting going. 'Mush' comes from the French word *marcais*, which means 'to march on.''

'The commands we do use,' continued Erin, stroking Ruda's head beside her, 'are 'gee' which means right, 'ha' which means left, and 'whoa' which means stop. We use 'onby' when another team is about to cross in the opposite direction.'

'Have you ever won the Iditarod?' asked someone standing nearby, admiring her sledge.

'Oh, no,' laughed Erin, 'we've never won anything. My husband is famous for adding fifty miles to every race he's in.'

Getting lost is a big problem in races like these it appears, and Erin told us about the uncanny ability of the husky lead dog to 'remember' a race route. 'About the hardest thing of being a musher,' said Erin, 'is to put complete trust in your lead dog. He knows where the trail is. He remembers!'

She told us a few stories of how the lead dog had insisted on the opposite direction when she had chosen another route, one that had been marked by the officials, albeit incorrectly.

Erin herself has not done the Iditarod but has done the Serum Race three times. They are busy preparing for her husband to tackle next year's Iditarod.

There are many hidden dangers in the wilderness. If the route is clear, Erin described how she would kneel on the back of the sledge and sleep on her hands for a few minutes at a time. Sometimes they run into other animals. A friend of hers had a big moose run into her dogs and got tangled up in the ropes. She had to kill it with her ice axe!

But it is man who is the biggest danger.

'Drunk snow-machiners are our worst enemy,' said Erin with a pained expression on her face.

Erin spoke about how the dogs just love the running and being part of the pack. Often when a dog is injured, they have to be put in the sledge itself and the injured dog howls itself silly to be put back into the team!

On the appointed day each February, on the corner of 4th and D road here in Anchorage, just across from the statue of Balto, the most famous of the dogs who carried the serum to Nome in 1925, the Iditarod race begins. Ninety or so teams of dogs head north into the Arctic winter, where the unique bond of dog and man has been demonstrated so acutely.

175

Here in Anchorage, alongside Erin McLarnon and her dog Ruda, it's clear that the bond between dog and woman is equally strong.

Our cruise ship docked in Anchorage this morning, and we've swapped the luxury of the cruise for a small rental car, and a long list of must-sees in the few weeks ahead. Jacky has spent many happy hours alongside the *beached whales* on the top deck loungers, reading *The Rough Guide to Alaska*, and her list has got longer each day. Puffins and Santa are not on her list yet, but I'm hoping to slip them in!

We never did meet our mysterious towel guy or girl, but we left him or her a happy note and an even happier gratuity!

ANCHORAGE   NORTH POLE

CHAPTER FORTY-THREE

Anybody can be Santa

North Pole, Alaska
August 1st — 64°45'17.05"N, 147°20'35.02"W

When travelling, it is wonderful to have the time and flexibility to spot an interesting place on a map, and on the spur of the moment, to go there. While my intention all along had been to find the Alaskan Santa, this was not something I had admitted to Jacky. I had to pretend it was fortuitous. Looking at the map together last night, my finger stopped on a very curious place.

'North Pole,' it said. It was about fifteen miles southeast of Fairbanks, but it said 'North Pole'.

Pretending it was the first I'd heard about it, I started to ask around, and someone nearby told us that Santa was there!

'But I thought you met Santa in Lapland?' said Jacky, looking at me strangely.

'I did,' I said, 'that's why I'm so confused.'

I grinned at her. 'There can't be two Santa's, can there?'

We hightailed it north, nearly two hundred miles out of our way, switching the radio channels all the way there. There were plenty of country music choices here, much to my delight, and less so to Jacky! A little after six on a Sunday evening, we arrived on the outskirts of North Pole, Alaska. Now North Pole is pretty far north as places go, but 'this was a bit ridiculous', I thought, as we encountered all manner of street and business signs proclaiming that Santa was indeed here. Santa Claus Lane, St. Nicholas Drive, Kris Kringle Drive, Snowman Lane, Holiday Lane, even Santaland RV Park – it was all here. The local radio station is KJNP (King Jesus North Pole).

Formerly a district of Fairbanks, it became a separate town in 1953 and was named North Pole in the hope of attracting manufacturers who could then say *Manufactured at North Pole* on their labels. It didn't bring the manufacturers, but it did bring Santa.

We arrived at Santa Claus House, on Santa Claus Lane, and parked beneath a forty-foot-high fibreglass statue of Santa. We, however, were interested in the real thing.

'Surprise, surprise, season's greetings,' called Santa to us as we entered Santa Claus House. He was sitting on a big throne, surrounded by Christmas trees and presents. He wore a blue T-shirt that stretched out to accommodate his big stomach and on his head, of course, he had a red hat. What was most impressive of Santa, however, was his beard – a long, white beard that was his very own.

'Season's greetings all the way from the North Pole,' said Santa as I moved closer to him, Jacky hovering with the camera not far away, capturing the moment.

I didn't waste time with formalities – I plunged right in.

'Santa,' I said, giving him the benefit of the doubt, 'I'm confused. I thought Santa lived in Lapland.'

He smiled at me disarmingly. Gee, these Santa's were good.

'Well, that's true,' he said, 'Oh yes, I know there's a Santa Claus in Lapland.' Then he paused and leaned towards me, about to impart a secret. 'You see,' he said, 'there are many people that love to strive to spread the love of the man upstairs – because it's Jesus' birthday – it's what Christmas is all about.'

That wasn't quite the answer I was expecting.

He picked up a nearby card and pointed to where he had signed his name. 'You'll notice that whenever I sign something, I do the T in the shape of a cross.'

I wasn't falling for all this. 'Tell me about your elves,' I said, looking around for a protégée of Pete's.

Santa pointed up to a giant sledge suspended in the air. Plastic elves were hanging over the edge. 'There are some genuine artificial replicas,' he said.

Genuine artificial replicas?

'But where are the real elves?' I insisted.

'Oh, I've got hundreds of them,' said Santa, 'they're busy building the toys for the children. I get to go and spread the love and happiness. They make the toys.'

'So they don't get out at all?' I spluttered, knowing the real truth of course.

'Oh, they're satisfied where they're at,' said Santa, 'they're very happy.'

I left it at that. Santa rambled on a bit about how the elves don't just get fed porridge, but also lots of glout and lots of mush. Glout, he explained, is kind-of-like grits, which are ground up corn. Sounds like porridge to me. So does mush. Lucky elves.

For my final question, I asked how he delivered all the presents at the same time. He answered immediately; the words just flowed out. 'Magic...love,' he said, 'and I have a lot of other helpers out there who strive to go and spread the love and happiness. Because, you know, anybody who is willing to help, anybody is able to be Santa. All you have to do is care and to go and give, just to create a smile and a twinkle in a child's eye. And a child can be anyone from one day old to a hundred and twenty years.'

We left him there, Santa, alone in his chair, staring at the front entrance, waiting for another child.

I like that one quote – 'Anybody is able to be Santa'.

I really do.

It makes me want to believe.

We left him there, Santa, alone in his chair, staring at the front entrance, waiting for another child.

I like that one quote – 'anybody is able to be Santa.'

NORTH POLE

SANCTUARY RIVER

CHAPTER FORTY-FOUR

How Not to Find a Grizzly

Sanctuary River, Denali National Park
August 3rd — 63°39'30.65"N, 149°47'53.57"W

'Hello Mister Bear,' called Jacky loudly as we gingerly pushed our way through the undergrowth, struggling to find the path. Just out of sight, the glacial waters of the Sanctuary River swept past, making gurgling and rushing sounds over the smooth pebbles that lined the river.

'Hello Mister Bear,' I called a moment or two later as I pushed the low hanging spruce branch away from my face.

There are two ways to find bears in the Alaskan wilderness. The first is to creep quietly along deserted forest paths until, in time, you stumble upon a very surprised bear. The second, and least useful in terms of actually finding bears, is to make as much noise as possible. The 'Hello Mister Bear' part was our little addition to this second option.

Camping in Denali National Park, Alaska, where there are no fences, and the bears roam free, is an exciting and exhilarating experience. Jacky lugged a tent, cool box and sleeping bag all the way from South Africa, which must be a record for long distance camping. En route we visited one of the many Alaskan Fishing and Hunting mega stores and bought a blow-up mattress to provide some comfort, a small camping stove and a children's fishing rod in case we found salmon. Our rental car has been great for exploring the byways of Alaska and led us last night to a campground at Byers Lake, a small lake surrounded by spruce. We swam in the cold water in the evening and again in the morning, where we were joined by two trumpeter swans and their four offspring and a mother duck with twenty ducklings.

At the entrance to Denali, the Serengeti of Alaska, as it is sometimes referred to, we were given strict instructions and even shown a demonstration video on how to deal with bears.

There are two types of bears in Denali – the smaller black bear and the larger grizzly (North American brown bear). The instructions on how to deal with them go something like this:

1) If you are out in the wilderness, make a lot of noise. Bears have excellent hearing and will usually hear you long before you see them, and get out of your way.

2) Never run from a bear! Bears can run faster than fifty kilometres an hour, and they will often chase anything that runs from them. (Hmm...)

3) If a grizzly approaches, speak in a low, calm voice while waving your arms above your head. If it charges you, stand still. Do not run. (Sure!)

4) If a black bear approaches you, be aggressive, shout at it, and throw things at it to make it go away.

5) If a grizzly attacks you, fall to the ground, curl up in a ball, with your hands around the back of your neck, and play dead.

6) If a black bear attacks you, fight back.

Would you go off into the wilderness after all that?

It was mid-afternoon when the green camper bus from Denali dropped us off at Sanctuary River campsite, a small area with only two other campers. We pitched our tent and then, armed with a small backpack, a fishing rod and a can of anti-bear pepper spray (our last line of defence), we set off for a hike up the river and found ourselves wandering along a forested bank beside the river, expecting a bear attack at any moment.

After about a half hour of calling to Mister Bear, we began to relax and followed the river to the southeast and began to find spoor alongside the river. First, it was moose spoor, giant half-moon shapes set deep in the mud, and then, finally, the unmistakeable print of a bear. We looked around immediately, of course, invoking a dozen 'Hello Mister Bear's', but there was no response.

We stood there for a long time, in the late afternoon, taking in the spectacle of the wide flowing river, the spruce-lined mountains to the west, the noise of the gurgling water and the views out over the eastern tundra. It was a real moment to remember.

The term 'tundra' refers both to a landscape where below zero temperatures are prevalent and also to the open plains where the ground is covered by grasses and clumps of low bushes. Many of these bushes

181

hold the delicate berries that are the favourite of the grizzly. Grizzlies tend to hang out in the open tundra, much like the caribou, while the smaller black bear, like the moose, tends to favour the forests.

Because of the long, cold winters and the inability of the land to support large numbers of game, the tundra is relatively empty of wildlife. With the animals widely spread, the excitement and appreciation of sightings are enhanced.

There were no fishing holes in the fast-flowing river, so we headed for the undulating ground of the tundra where we continued to call for Mister Bear, pepper spray at the ready. Each crest or ridge was climbed in trepidation and exhilaration, a confrontation with a nine-foot, thousand pound grizzly expected constantly. But we were not so lucky...

On the opposite hillside, we did spot a beautiful caribou with big antlers covered in velvet. Caribou are the wild version of the reindeer and together with the moose, are the primary ungulates in Alaska.

After nearly three hours of enjoyable hiking, we found ourselves a little lost, but some neat orienteering brought us back to the road and the sighting of a family of surprised willow ptarmigan that flew out from under a bush as we passed. Willow ptarmigan are brown game birds that change to white during winter, like the arctic hare and the arctic fox – the perfect disguise in the snow.

We returned to our campsite under the spruce trees, and before the sun disappeared behind the mountain, we cooked a dinner of spaghetti bolognaise on our new camping stove, opened a bottle of carefully packed red wine and listened to the noises of the tundra and the water of the Sanctuary River in front of us. As the temperature dropped, we zipped ourselves inside our little tent and listened for bears.

'Hello Mister Bear,' we called once or twice, this time in jest.

It's easy to be brave when you're safe.

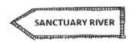

CHAPTER FORTY-FIVE

A Bear, a Bus Driver, a Hobbit and a Big ol' Camper Bus

Wonder Lake, Denali National Park
August 4th — 63°27'55.10"N, 150°52'12.62"W

'My name is still Dick,' said the bus driver, 'and this is still the 8.30 camper bus.' He looked at us in his wide rear-view mirror, watching for expressions of mirth. Immediately in front of us, between ourselves and Dick, came a jolly little laugh from an unseen person.

The time was just after 9.40 am, the appointed time when the 8.30 green camper bus from Denali headquarters trundled past our campsite along Sanctuary River. We had spent a cold night in our little tent and this morning found our towels, which we'd left outside, turned into sheets of ice. The camper bus stopped for us on a lonely road lined by spruce trees, and we loaded up our backpacks, tent, sleeping bags, cool box and fishing pole, and settled in for the ride to the far end of the park, to a romantic sounding place called Wonder Lake.

I stood up and identified the source of the jolly little laugh. It was a very short person, a woman of about forty, with coke bottle glasses and tiny shrunken hands.

'Dick's good,' she said to me in greeting. 'He'll find us bears,' she said confidently.

'Good,' I replied, sitting back in my seat. The woman disappeared from view.

Despite the cold of the night before, it was a beautiful day, without a cloud in the sky and the contrast of the forests, the high mountain ranges and the deep blue sky reminded me of scenes from the movie *The Lord of the Rings*.

It was when the small woman stood in the aisle to talk to a friend further back in the bus, that I began to wonder whether she might not be a person after all, and might, in fact, be a hobbit. She was about four foot seven high and as round as a button, with a small mouth and a curious nose. As she stood there in the aisle, biting into a red pepper, I nodded quietly to myself.

A hobbit indeed.

From Sanctuary River, Dick and his big ol' camper bus took us through a range of varied scenery – from open plains that stretched to distant mountains, to forests of spruce, to rocky passes that dropped hundreds of metres to glacial riverbeds. It was terrific viewing, but without that one key component – animals. We did spot two caribou, but Dick and Hobbitgirl didn't show much interest. They were far too engrossed in a lively discussion about Mount McKinley, the tallest mountain in North America, its snow-covered top just visible in the distance.

Hobbitgirl was fascinated by colour, we soon realised, and photography. Everything she said was couched in the language of light.

'What nice contrast,' she'd said at the sight of open plains set against dark forests. 'What a great angle,' she'd said when a glacial riverbed made a sharp turn in the mountains.

Dick wasn't interested in contrasts and angles, nor had he contributed to much active game spotting which, as it happened, seemed to fall to Jacky and I, who had each spotted a caribou inside the first hour.

Instead, Dick, the driver, rambled on about the exact height of Mount McKinley, the distance between its north and south peaks and its comparison to Mount Nangasomething somewhere in Pakistan where Dick ventured, the political climate was not so good.

'Oooh, look at the greens and yellows,' squeaked the small-mouthed hobbit as we crested a rise and looked out over a vast, open expanse.

'Caribou at three o'clock,' called out Jacky, pointing at the beautiful deer with its magnificent antlers, lying contentedly in the low bushes.

'Yes,' said Dick, the driver, 'a caribou.'

He stared in contemplation at the caribou for a moment, then continued, 'Now, Mount McKinley is also known as Mount Denali. Denali means 'the great one.''

In front of us, Hobbitgirl pointed up into the sky and cried out, 'Oh blue – blue, blue, blue, blue, blue,' and then took a breath and uttered a final, 'blue, blue'.

It was at this point that I began to suffer flashbacks to safari drives in Africa, where other passengers were intently focused on birds, or trees, or something obscure, while I was set on the more predictable

Big Five. In Alaska, the Big Five is the caribou, the moose, the Dall sheep, the wolf and, of course, the bear, and so far, we had only seen one of the five. So it was that we began to be frustrated by the antics of Hobbitgirl and Dick, the driver.

When we saw the mountain for about the tenth time, Hobbitgirl decided the time was right for a photograph. Dick didn't agree.

'We'll see it much closer a bit later on,' he said.

'How about now?' said Hobbitgirl, thirty seconds later. Dick did not stop and mumbled something at the mountain.

'How about now?' she said again, about twenty seconds later, and this time Dick screeched the bus to a halt in frustration and unleashed an orgy of photography, comments on colours and mountain talk.

In the seat behind Hobbitgirl, Jacky and I politely chewed on our tongues and thought of returning home in shame, with a lone caribou our only conquest of the Alaskan Big Five.

Twenty minutes later, Dick stopped the bus for a rest stop, in full view of the mountain. Hobbitgirl joined us on the ridge and proceeded to educate us on the secrets of landscape painting. I realised, with a little shame, that she was not a hobbit, but a really interesting art teacher from New York.

With us positioned on each shoulder, she cupped her hands and framed Mount McKinley between her stubby fingers. Gently, she waved her hands in brushing strokes down the sides of the great mountain, imagining her paint dripping down along the sides of snow.

'See,' she said, and we nodded, appreciative for the first time. Then she showed us her sketchbook and how she planned a painting, from her earliest sketch to concepts like depth of vision and constructs of value and finally, to the masterpiece itself. But it was colour that she loved the most.

'I can see two hundred colours in your face,' she said to Jacky.

'Oh my,' said Jacky, lifting her hands to cover her cheeks and giving me a weird look. 'Oh no,' said Hobbitgirl, reaching up and patting Jacky's shoulder. 'Good colours, only good colours.'

When we boarded the bus, our impressions on Mount McKinley deepened with new insights, Dick, the driver, was in a dark mood.

'Where's your friend?' he snapped at Hobbitgirl, and we all looked back and saw her friend standing far away, staring out into space.

'Well, I said ten minutes,' said Dick, revving the engine and closing the doors, 'and ten minutes it is.'

In his defence, this was the third time that Hobbitgirl's vacuous friend had held up the bus at rest stops.

Hobbitgirl called out loudly in the bus, 'No Dick, you can't do that with her,' and insisted that he open the doors again while her friend casually strolled down the road towards us.

Jacky and I raised our eyebrows at each other. It was clear that relations between Hobbitgirl and Dick, the driver, had begun to cool.

'We're running late now,' said Dick loudly as he pulled off and drove on through even more beautiful scenery and reached the Polychrome Pass, a winding dirt road that hangs precariously high above the dry bed of the East Fork River.

Looking down the steep cliffside, and trying to ignore the effects of vertigo; at that most unlikely of moments, our grizzly arrived. After the many hours spent scanning the shores of Canada and Alaska from atop our cruise ship, to the clandestine and unsuccessful search for the Garbage Dump Bears of Hoonah Island, to yesterday's exhilarating bear hunt along the rocky shores of Sanctuary River – suddenly, unexpectedly, there he was, loping casually down the river bed. He was a huge bear, dark in the shadow of the mountain, his great paws sweeping forwards as he walked.

I saw him first.

'Yeah, that's a grizzly,' said Dick casually, amid a wild scramble for cameras. But he didn't stop the bus.

'We'll see him better from a bit further on,' he said, and our beloved bear disappeared from view as we rounded the bend. Sadly, 'a bit further on' proved a disaster as our great bear must have sat down, or turned around, something our bus could not do on the narrow road.

Even Hobbitgirl was disappointed. She mumbled something I could not quite make out.

'Grizzlies have such great colours,' it might have been.

Our big ol' camper bus headed off down the pass, leaving a trail of dust behind. On board, Dick, the driver, peered ahead in the hope of making amends, Hobbitgirl played with her camera in her tiny hands, and we sat back, elated at finding our grizzly at last, and a little sad at leaving so soon.

Hobbit girl was fascinated by colour, we soon realised,
and by photography. Everything she said was couched
in the language of light.
'What nice contrast,' she'd said at the sight of open
plains set against dark forests.
'What a great angle,' she'd said when a glacial riverbed
made a sharp turn in the mountains.

CHAPTER FORTY-SIX

Begging for Chocolate

Denali National Park, Alaska
August 5th — 63°27'55.10"N, 150°52'12.62"W

'Excuse me,' I said to a group of students from North Carolina who were busy eating their supper at Wonder Lake campground, last night. There were about ten of them, their mouths full, and they all looked up at me with questioning eyes.

'Sorry to bother you,' I said, feeling ridiculous, 'but my girlfriend is not able to function without something sweet to eat.'

A few of them smiled at me, standing there, cap in hand, so to speak.

'Do you have anything sweet?' I said, 'anything at all.'

They followed my eyes back to our nearby campsite, where Jacky was sitting at the wooden table beside our tent, using our camping stove to try and make caramel out of two little sugar sachets in a metal can.

Desperate times call for desperate measures.

The students were now all laughing, and one girl jumped up from the bench and beckoned me to follow, calling over her shoulder, 'You deserve chocolate for having the guts to come and ask.'

I didn't tell her that I'd been to two other groups before theirs.

From her bag, she retrieved a small bag of chocolate balls and gave me four of them. 'Seattle's best chocolate,' she called after me as I left them, and I raised my right hand in triumph, the balls between my fingers. Jacky was delighted with the chocolate, and also I think, that I'd been prepared to beg for it! Maybe I'm marriage material?

Camping has such simple pleasures.

That was last night. After our long bus drive with Dick, the driver and Hobbitgirl, we'd had a relaxing afternoon at the beautiful Wonder Lake, and camped on a hillside that overlooked a stunning plain and the snow-covered Mount Denali in the distance. We listened to a ranger talk about the wolves of Denali, and after supper and a little chocolate and burned sugar, listened to the sounds of the Alaskan night from inside our tent.

This morning we boarded the 6.30 green camper bus, bound for the return to Denali headquarters, a five-hour bus ride that we hoped would provide us with a better sighting of a grizzly. Hobbitgirl and her vacuous friend were there too, but the driver was different. Scott Richardson from Hawaii was our driver, a friendly fellow with an eye for spotting animals.

His first spot was a family of four beaver swimming happily alongside their nest in a dam beside the road. Jacky and I were very excited at our first sighting of these beautiful creatures with big teeth. Not far down the road, we saw our first moose of the day, a female, happily drinking from a lake. Then it was the turn of the grizzlies.

It was an overcast day, not too hot, and perfect for sitting out in the tundra, chewing on some berries. Amazingly, we saw five separate grizzlies, wandering riverbeds or munching on the berries of the tundra – blueberries, cranberries, cloudberries and crowberries. The grizzlies of Denali are distinctly blonde in colour, particularly on their backs. Their species name of Ursus Arctos Horribilis seemed inappropriate in the lovely morning sunshine.

As we drove and at each rest stop, we kept hearing the excited chatter of the drivers, rangers and field guides of Denali, about an Italian photojournalist who claimed to have been attacked by a grizzly, and who beat it off with an ice-pick, leaving the ice-pick protruding from the grizzly's head. We have now heard several conspiracy theories, and no one believes the Italian's story. He says he was filming caribou when the grizzly attacked him from behind. Just last week, this same journalist received a warning from rangers for going too close to bears. It seems likely that he was doing the same, probably filming a grizzly with cubs, and got way too close.

Denali is very proud of its safety record, and before this incident, they haven't had a grizzly attack for seven years. The bears keep out of the way of humans, don't associate them with food or danger, and focus instead on the berries and the occasional caribou. Meanwhile, the rangers are out in force, searching for an injured bear with an ice-pick in its head.

Driver Scott also spotted several groups of white Dall sheep high up in the hills, lots of caribous and, just when we thought we'd seen everything, he found us wolves. There are only about a hundred wolves in Denali, and the ones we found were from the Grant Creek Pack. We saw a beautiful black wolf (the alpha male) and his two pups, one of whom ran boisterously up to him, licking his face. The alpha female was apparently injured a few days ago while hunting caribou and is thought to be lying low in the nearby den. The wolves reminded me so much of the African wild dog, and, of course, of huskies.

Hobbitgirl was feeling a little poorly and had lost her voice, so we were deprived of her insights on the journey. Her name is Julie, and she comes from the Bronx in New York City. She has been in Alaska for over four weeks, two of which were at an art conference in Fairbanks.

Hobbitgirl's friend, however, continued her antics from the previous day, disappearing at every single rest stop, and waiting for driver Scott to come and find her, before consenting to get on the bus again. Once on the bus, she would go to sleep, often in a ridiculous position. When we found the wolves and everyone clambered all over the bus to take photographs, she slept with her face up against the back of our seat.

Jacky and I think there is something wrong with her.

Midway through the bus trip, she decided to get off the bus altogether and have 'a little lie down'. She is probably still there, alone with the bears and wolves of Denali.

We left Denali and headed south again, aiming for a place called Homer, on the peninsula below Anchorage, and were quite desperate to catch a salmon.

We also stocked up on chocolate and were both in excellent spirits.

 DENALI HQ  HOMER SPIT

CHAPTER FORTY-SEVEN

Horned Puffins and a Deckhand called Jeff

Kachemak Bay, Homer, Alaska
August 6th — 59°36'17.81"N, 151°25'32.78"W

'Hi,' said Jacky, fluttering her eyelids at the four men standing idle on the small wooden walkway above Willow Creek. I watched from a distance, leaving this messy business of currying favour with the locals to the expert.

I couldn't hear much of the conversation, but she must have been convincing for the four men quickly surrounded her, and began to show her how to set up our fishing rod to catch salmon.

I edged a little nearer.

'You need a very small sinker,' said a man with a big stomach, 'Here – have one of mine.' Niftily he attached the sinker to the line, while a short, stocky man helped Jacky choose the right lure from the little collection we had bought.

'Red's good,' commented the third man, and the fourth, staring at Jacky's breasts, added, 'Yes, nice and shiny.'

There are not many pretty women in Alaska.

Then began the lecture on the secret fishing holes and channels of Willow Creek, and a little later, Jacky and I hitched up our trousers and waded through the stream to an island in the middle, from where the men had promised Jacky, 'You'll be sure to catch a silver.'

The silver salmon were leaping out the water at us as we crossed, coming upstream in schools of about ten at a time, their glittering sides teasing us as we argued about who would use the rod first.

Every thirty seconds or so one would leap out the water, and crash back with a great splash, jerking our heads towards the offending spot.

Jacky got the rod first. She deserved it after her performance with the four Alaskan men. I was just being difficult and over eager to fish.

It didn't matter. Both of us were hopeless.

We'd cast carefully out in front of the swimming salmon, then slowly reel in the lure, drawing it past them as they swam. As these salmon, heading for their spawning beds and death, have long since stopped feeding, the only way to catch one was to irritate them with the lure until they snapped at it and hooked themselves.

As we traded turns (ten casts each), eventually Jacky learned to count, but by then both the salmon and the men watching us lost interest and left, the salmon to swim upstream to spawn and the men downstream to the Willow Creek pub.

Predictably, a small boy from the village popped down for a spot of fishing after his dinner and snagged a big salmon of about six pounds straight away. Casually he killed it with a rock, slung it over his shoulder and without even a glance in our direction, headed for home.

We were defeated.

We trudged back to the car, bemoaning our equipment, each other, the little red lure - anything but our skill - and headed off on a night safari on a deserted Alaskan road, trying to redeem our day. We did, in some measure, for we found four different North American porcupines, waddling beside the road.

Since our first stop on the cruise ship, that visit to Ketchikan, where Jacky had stolen the rod and spoiled the child, we have been diligently trying to catch our first salmon.

At a place called Moose Creek, not far south of Denali, we stopped on a bridge and looked down on a tranquil stream, boiling with king salmon, their bodies a deep red colour. Two of them were already dead, and a small boy played on the bank, oblivious to bears. At other rivers we watched in amazement at the many anglers lining the banks, taking advantage of Alaska's salmon run. And in Denali, armed with our fishing pole, pepper spray and our lungs full of 'Hello Mister Bear' breath, we'd hiked up Sanctuary River in search of grizzlies and places to fish. We'd found neither.

And that brought us to Homer, a delightful town on the southwestern corner of the grand peninsula that juts out below Anchorage. Homer is set in spectacular surroundings, on the waters of Kachemak Bay. With snow-covered mountains framing the town and the spires of three volcanoes in the distance, it's the perfect setting for the halibut fishing capital of the world, as Homer is known.

Halibut is a large flat fish, brown on top and white below, and feeds in big shoals near the ocean floor off the Alaskan coast.

We arrived here last night, determined to catch a fish, and hopefully to find a puffin!

A cousin of the Atlantic puffin can be found nearby, according to my co-conspirator from 'The Great Icelandic Puffin Hunt', Robbo.

'*The horned puffin,*' emailed Robbo, a.k.a. Professor Puffin, '*is so distinctive by its white breast, that in one Eskimo language, they are called 'katukhpule', meaning 'big white breast.''* Robbo's research further revealed that the horned puffin is probably the most easily recognised of Alaska's seabirds and, like most of the puffins of Iceland, Scotland and Norway, they nest in sheer cliffs on uninhabited islands just off the coast.

Knowing how disappointed Robbo would be if I did not find the horned puffins of Kachemak Bay, and how disappointed Jacky would be if she did not catch a fish, I nervously approached the frizzy blonde lady manning the desk advertising fishing trips on the small boat, Trailerbuster II.

She nodded and said, 'Of course,' when I asked about fishing the next day for halibut and perhaps salmon, but looked at me blankly when I asked, 'Would the captain also be able to find puffins for us?'

After working my charm on her for a while (Jacky is not the only one with charm), she phoned the captain at home, interrupting his dinner to ask about puffins.

A little later, faced with the choice of looking for puffins or having no customers at all, the captain agreed.

'He'll find you puffins,' beamed the frizzy blonde at me.

'And fishing?' asked Jacky.

'And fishing,' said the frizzy blonde.

Early today we drove out onto Homer Spit, a narrow four-mile-long, low-lying peninsula that juts out into Kachemak Bay. We boarded Trailerbuster II, a fishing launch designed for twelve, but fortunately only carrying six today, plus the captain and a deckhand called Jeff.

'We are also doing a bit of birdwatching today folks,' said Captain Weldon Chivers, pointing me out to a group of four Americans from Nevada who had come all the way here for some serious fishing.

He needn't have pointed. I was the only one carrying a large, cuddly, puffin toy. I'd picked it up in a souvenir shop the previous day. It had sort of jumped out at me.

'I brought it just in case Weldon didn't know what one looked like,' I said, a bit embarrassed, staring back at these most serious of fishermen.

Everyone, Jacky included, stared back at me as if I had completely lost my mind.

From rock bottom, things could only improve. We headed out into Kachemak Bay on a beautiful sunlit morning, with blue skies stretching to the horizon, the sea like glass and the domes of the volcanoes brooding down at us. While the Americans sat in the cabin and spoke of halibut and politics, Jacky and I stood at the back of the boat, scanning for wildlife and, in particular, puffins.

Amazingly, first up were two sea otters, lazily playing in the water, their silky, smooth bodies gliding and twisting on the surface. After my failed search for the otter of Rum, and my mistaken sighting of the Bermudan sea otter, finding the real thing was quite a feeling.

As we moved further out to sea, we began to encounter more and more seabirds, clustered in little groups on the water, all of them gulls of some variety. Then, without bidding from the captain, I spotted a familiar shape bobbing on the water – a puffin. The little bird, with a yellow and orange beak, peered at us curiously for a moment, then dived beneath the surface, no doubt heading for the distant bottom and its next meal of sand eels.

It wasn't long before the sky and sea were full of puffins, and my enthusiasm had everyone out on deck admiring my little friends. They were horned puffins, similar in appearance to the Atlantic puffin, and named for a black 'horn' that points up from the top of its eye.

'I've been coming here for years,' said one of the Americans, 'and I never knew what a puffin was.'

He looked around him as if discovering a new world.

'Well, I never,' he said to no one in particular. It was clear that their opinion of me had now changed. But it was time to fish, and Jeff, the deckhand, was the main man. A big guy, with a very flexible face and a goatee beard, Jeff was wearing a blue overall, and a happy smile. On the bumpy ride out he had amazed me with his dexterity as he baited up the hooks, rigged the rods and performed plenty of other boating necessities, all with sure-footed ease on a bouncing boat.

Jeff gave us each a short fishing rod, loaded up with a two-pound sinker and an enormous metal hook, and baited with enough fish to feed a hungry cat.

'Let them all the way down,' he ordered, and we fed out our line until the sinker hit the bottom with a thud.

It wasn't long before the first fish bit, and we enjoyed the heavy task of hauling the big halibut in, one after the other.

From a nearby boat a pistol shot rang out, and we watched them haul an enormous halibut aboard.

'They have to shoot the real big ones,' explained Jeff, 'otherwise they'll hurt someone in the boat.'

Between us, Jacky and I caught twelve halibut and a large sting-ray. Because of quotas, we could only keep the four largest halibut, which were each between twenty and thirty pounds, and the others were released.

'Now that we've all got our quota,' said the captain ('and seen the horned puffins,' I thought), 'we might try our hand for some salmon.'

Jacky beamed.

As we moved closer inshore, Jeff armed each of us with a lighter rod, baited with a colourful lure. The secret, Jeff told us, was to drop the lure to a depth of about forty feet and then to raise the rod up and down, creating the illusion of a small fish streaking through the water. The salmon in these waters, yet to make their journey into the fresh water of the Alaskan rivers, were still in feeding mode.

After about twenty minutes of no success, it was clear that the salmon were not going to be as obliging as the halibut. When my salmon struck, the rod dipped hard, and the brief fight gave me a great thrill. It was a beautiful pink salmon, also known as a humpy, and weighed about seven pounds.

After another hour, Jacky had still not caught a salmon, but just as we were about to give up and head for Homer, her line ran, and with a big grin on her face, her cheeks flushed with excitement and suntan, she brought her fish in.

As she held it up for me to photograph beside her beaming smile, I could not help remember our fishing tribulations in getting here.

Our fish we donated to the Americans, who come here annually and take their catch back home. It keeps them stocked for most of the year. We did, however, make two exceptions:

Firstly, we had Jeff cut each of us a sliver of our salmon, and on the open deck, with the spray of the sea in our faces, we had our very own Alaskan sashimi.

Secondly, we kept back two of the halibut fillets and on return to Homer, took it to the local fish and chips shop, where they cooked them for us.

It was Jacky's last evening in Alaska – her time as part of this adventure was ending, and in the excitement of travel, and the search for bears, puffins, Santas and salmon, we've hardly spoken of what the future might hold for us together.

In the late evening, on the narrow Homer Spit, we sat at a green plastic table beside the sea, and ate our halibut with our fingers, marvelling at how fortunate we were, as two little people in this great and wonderful world, to be doing the things we do.

CHAPTER FORTY-EIGHT

The Blonde Puffins of Resurrection Bay

Alaska SeaLife Center, Seward, Alaska
August 8th — 60°05'59.70"N, 149°26'27.67"W

Watching a bird in flight is a mesmerising experience – its graceful movements through the air, its poise, and its remarkable ability to glide in the wind, effortlessly changing direction in an instant.

This morning I watched in awe, standing with my mouth open as a chubby bird with a bright beak flew gracefully past me, underneath the water, its blonde hair trailing behind it!

I looked around in amazement to see if anyone else had seen what I had just witnessed. But no, I was alone. The other people in the basement were watching a Stellar sea lion swim around in its tank; its big eyes staring back at them.

I was at the Alaska SeaLife Center in Seward, a small town two hours south of Anchorage and had come to see the tufted puffins of Resurrection Bay. Jacky and I said our goodbyes yesterday at Anchorage airport, in a surreal scene where she gradually disappeared, down a distant escalator. With a lump in my throat, I turned and went looking for puffins.

My intrigue with the fat little puffin might have begun in Iceland, but it had gathered momentum in the Isle of Rum, in Norway and two days ago in Kachemak Bay, Alaska. With the Atlantic puffin and the horned puffin carefully marked off in my Moleskine notebook, I came to Seward in search of the tufted puffin and my hat-trick in the puffin world. The tufted puffin is a curious bird with an all-black body and two tufts of blonde hair, each two to three inches long, beginning just to the side of each ear and flowing back down its neck.

The Alaska SeaLife Center was paid for out of reparations from the 1989 Exxon Valdez oil disaster in nearby Prince William Sound and focuses on research, rehabilitation and public education. The exhibit of specific interest to me was that of the seabirds, an above ground aviary and rockery and a twenty-one-foot deep pool with a sandy bottom and lots of fish. Two sides of the pool are glassed, and from the basement of the center, one can watch in awe, as I did, as the tufted puffins dive beneath the surface and fly around the tank.

In the air, the puffin is an abysmal flyer who, on take-off, will often run on the water with its big webbed feet for about ten metres before either lifting off or crashing back into the water. Its wings beat an incredible forty times per second.

Underwater, the puffin comes into its own. Watching it beating its wings under the water, in the slow, measured manner that so drew me to the gulls of the skies, my only homage could be my jaw that hung down in complete amazement.

Determined to see a tufted puffin in the wild, I left the Sealife Center and wandered down to the harbour to try and convince a regular tourist boat's crew to find me a tufted puffin. At the information office, a helpful girl called Zoey promised me puffins, and as I left for the boat, she called after me,

'So, are you a birder?'

I looked at her for a moment.

'No, I'm a puffiner,' and laughed at my own very small joke.

About an hour into the cruise, the captain brought the boat into Emerald Cove, one of the many inlets of the spectacular Resurrection Bay, a fjord riven aeons ago by enormous glaciers. Sheer cliffs, several hundred metres high, hung precariously overhead as the captain nosed the boat within metres of the cliffs.

I stood up front in the open, right at the bow of the boat, pretending I was all alone (with Robbo at my side), searching for puffins.

'There,' said the captain, pointing at a diagonal cleft in the rock, about five metres above the surface. 'A tufted puffin.'

And it was.

The shy little puffin stared back at us, its blonde locks looking ridiculous. Suddenly from out to sea, its mate came hurtling in on the wind, wings working furiously. It landed badly in the cleft, tumbling about and distracting its mate from our approach.

Over the loudspeaker, the captain told of seeing a puffin fly straight into a rock face, and break its neck.

Over the next few minutes, we spotted several other tufted puffins, and I returned to Seward very pleased with myself and enriched by other sightings of bald eagles, Stellar sea lions and several glaciers.

Remembering my morning enchantment, I returned to the SeaLife Center for one last time, for another glimpse of my underwater flying heroes. They didn't disappoint.

At about twenty five centimetres high, the tufted puffin is slightly larger than the Atlantic and horned puffins and several million of them live along the Pacific Rim, from Japan all the way to mid-California. Its big difference from other puffins though is the depth of its dive. Incredibly, the tufted puffin can reach depths of three hundred feet, 'flying' all the way.

There are six tufted puffins at the Alaska SeaLife Center, and I watched them for a very long time this afternoon. I didn't want to leave, but eventually, as I made my way to the exit, something stopped me.

'Excuse me,' I said to the man at the reception desk, his stomach bulging over his belt, 'do your puffins have names?'

'Excuse me?' he responded.

I repeated my question.

'No, I don't think so,' he said.

My journalistic instinct was now pricked.

'But you're not sure?' I said, nodding my head at him slowly.

'No, not really,' he admitted, meeting my eyes, 'why don't you ask upstairs?'

I did.

'No, I don't think so,' said the friendly girl at the discovery pool, where children of all ages can feel their way from starfish to anemones, 'and the girl who looks after the puffins has gone home.'

This still wasn't enough for me.

'Doesn't she keep notes?' I asked. 'Maybe she has a puffin file?'

Friendlygirl looked at me weirdly, but then actually tried to help me.

We went into the office, and against all expectation, found a file named *Seabirds*. Grinning broadly, I took the file and went and sat in the cafeteria. Midway through, I found even more than I hoped for...

These then are the tufted puffins of the Alaska SeaLife Center:

HARRIET – aka Harry or Harriet the Horrible – she was once thought to be a male, but after DNA testing, we changed her name. Her mate is puffin # 8.

PUFFIN # 8 – mate to Harriet.

JEN – named after one of the mammologists, she is paired with Tobin and nests in a burrow in the right-hand back corner.

TOBIN – boyfriend of Jen.

TRAILER TRASH – named such because she always looks a little ruffled. She has short tufts and has a black tip at the end of her beak. Her mate is Fabio, and they are very affectionate with each other all year round.

FABIO – was named because of his looks, he has very long tufts that touch his back. He is one of the oldest puffins we have. He is blind in one eye and walks around very slowly.

Ecstatic with my find, I took Puffingirl's file back to Friendlygirl and showed her the names. She looked at me as if I was mad.

'You do know they won't come to you when you call their names?' she said, looking worried.

I looked at her as if she was mad, and gave her a long, slow 'Yeeees'.

Later, sitting in a little pub in the forest, with the sign outside saying *Cheap Beer, Lousy Food*, I reflected on Friendlygirl's reaction, and remembered a similar response from Pimplehead, in the tiny museum in Honningsväg, Norway:

'Puffins are birds, just birds,' he'd said, as he left me....

FABIO & TRAILER TRASH

CHAPTER FORTY-NINE

The Once Rare Alaskan Sea Otter

Seward, Alaska
August 9th — 60°06'15.00"N, 149°26'32.00"W

About two hundred years ago, a beautiful mother sea otter stared up with big, surprised eyes, clutching her baby to her chest. She was nearly seven feet long, and her fur was thick and sleek, protecting her in these chilling waters. Ultimately though, it would cost her her life. Surrounding her were the kayaks of the local Aleut peoples, their bodies and heads covered in the fur of caribou, moose and bear. In their hands their oars were weapons. One of the hunters, however, wore a hat made from the pelt of a sea otter. He was a white man, with a big moustache and dark eyes.

'There she is, get her,' he shouted in Russian at the Aleuts, pointing at the otter, its head twisting on the surface. As the kayaks came closer, she dove beneath the water, feeling the swish of an oar nearby.

She dove deep and swam hard to get away from the men, but her baby could not stay under the water as long as she could. It needed air. She rose to the surface. Again the kayaks came for her, driving her under again and again. Eventually, exhausted, she surfaced for the final time.

The Aleuts passed the body of the mother back to the Russian, who grunted in approval. The baby otter was left to drown. The Aleuts shared stolen glances of shame. This was not how they had been taught to honour nature. For centuries their ancestors had hunted the sea otter, but with reverence, and not exploitation. Never would a mother otter be taken. The implications for the next generation of otters and Aleuts were just too obvious, the insult against nature too great.

Far, far away, in the capitals of Europe, the discovery of the fur of the sea otter in the mid-eighteenth century had transformed the world's fashion industry. Soft gold, it was called. In distant Alaska, until the late 1860's the territory of Russia, the exploitation and virtual slavery of the native Alaskans – Aleuts, Tlingits, Athapascans and others – had begun. Between 1741 and the early 1900's, over three million sea otters were killed for their pelts and brought to the very edge of extinction.

In the early 1900's, with the sea otter and many other species on the edge of extinction, man began to intervene and prevented the continued slaughter. Trade in sea otter pelts was outlawed, as was hunting, and in areas such as the Aleutian Islands, the reintroduction of the sea otter began. Today there are about fifty thousand northern sea otters in Alaskan and Canadian waters, and about fifteen thousand in Russia. Further south, the southern sea otter lives along the Californian coast and numbers around two and a half thousand. There are no, and never have been, any sea otters in Bermuda.

Today, here in the southern port of Seward, Alaska, I began my very own search for a sea otter. Jacky and I had spotted two sea otters during our fishing and puffin expedition in Kachemak Bay a few days ago, and I was determined to get a closer look at one.

'Keep an eye out for Oscar,' said Marlee, the owner of the little B&B where I stayed in Seward. 'He's always hanging out near the harbour.'

I didn't find Oscar at the harbour, midst the fishing and tourist boats, but to my great thrill, I did spot him about a mile further up the coast and watched him for a long time in my binoculars, a big smile of appreciation on my face.

The most compelling thing about a sea otter is their little face, so human-like in appearance, like that of a tiny old man wrapped in furs, or a newborn baby scrunching up its face in a scream.

Sea otters, the smallest marine mammal, have the densest fur in the animal kingdom, and are the only mammal, apart from primates, to make use of tools. The sea otter is often seen lying on its back in the water, resting a rock on its belly, which it uses to break open mussels and other shellfish. It is a voracious eater and can eat up to a third of its body weight in a single day – crabs, octopus, fish, mussels and clams. Like the tufted puffins, the sea otter can dive to a depth of around three hundred feet, although they tend to prefer shallower waters.

The sea otter relies entirely on its fur for protection against the cold, and any damage to its fur, such as from the effects of oil, can be fatal. The Exxon Valdez disaster in Prince William Sound killed around three thousand sea otters, with nearly eight hundred victims being found in a single area. The terrible effects of the disaster on marine birds, mammals and fish notwithstanding, its long-term impact is a little brighter. Many millions of dollars in reparations and voluntary contributions have been ploughed into rehabilitation centers like the Alaskan SeaLife Center at Seward, into more detailed research on the Alaskan marine ecosystem, and into education.

The sea otters of the world today are no longer endangered. They roam free, a protected species living in relative harmony with man – oil spills, gill nets and indigenous hunting notwithstanding. They are an inspiring creature that makes me appreciate the spectacular world in which I live.

Midst the stream of never-ending bad news about our world, I think of all those puffins in the world, inhabiting protected islands; I think of the sea otters and the grizzlies, the parrot fish of Bermuda and the polar bears, the Rum ponies and the Highland cattle. I think of the salmon returning to spawn, the humpback whales breaching out the water and the reindeer wandering free. It's a beautiful world.

As I wandered off to the B&B, I looked back one final time at Oscar, rolling about in the light swells of Resurrection Bay. I could have sworn he was smiling.

Midst the stream of never ending bad news about the world, I think of all those puffins in the world, inhabiting protected islands; I think of the sea otters and grizzlies, the parrot fish and the polar bears, the Rum ponies and the Highland cattle. I think of the salmon returning to spawn, the humpback whales breaching out of the water and the reindeer wandering free.

It's a beautiful world!

CHAPTER FIFTY

Rolling Stone Raggi

Seward, Alaska
August 9th — 60°06'15.00"N, 149°26'32.00"W

The greatest pleasure of travelling, I have found these past months, has been the ability to change plans at the last moment and go somewhere entirely different. That freedom of spirit took me to the Isle of Rum, sought out Santa in Lapland and found me the puffins. In enjoying these diversions, I have wondered whether it is possible to live one's life by this premise, or whether, like the rolling stone without moss, one was doomed to pass life by without ever finding a home.

And my wonderings have taken me back to Raggi, the girl with the dimply smile and the Norwegian chuckle. In *Raggi of Rum*, I wrote about all the interesting jobs that Raggi did on the Isle of Rum - from pony gilly to postlady to winkle picker to tour guide. She also worked in a slaughterhouse in Iceland processing five hundred sheep a day and drove an ice cream van around the Peak district in England. If that's not enough she worked as a ski lift operator in Reykjavik, for the police in Lancashire, for a bank in northern Norway, packed vegetables in Preston, prepared sandwiches in Norway and worked for Norwegian national television.

I've kept in touch with Raggi by email since leaving Greenland. One of her first emails announced that she had been fired from her job as the tour guide in Kulusuk, Greenland. The manager who fired her was that very same hotel manager who had resisted serving me food that hungry evening in the snow.

'They thought I was constantly high on drugs because I am always so happy,' wrote Raggi. *'And being so happy is apparently not 'normal', so they sacked me! They all believe I am a druggie-hippie now. Well, let them think that. I am happy, always, and I don't need any drugs! Haha. Unbelievable.'*

After leaving Greenland, Raggi spent some time backpacking in Iceland before moving on to the Faroe Islands for some more hitchhiking and camping. When she was through there, she wrote:

'I'm going up to northern Norway – Faroes was miserable, just loads of rain and my reindeer skin is about to rot. It really stinks. Yuck, but I just don't want to throw it away. Haha, must go, my stomach is rumbling. Cheers for now.'

In northern Norway, Raggi struck it rich. She expanded her little crochet hat business from Rum, and found the Norwegian market ripe for the taking, where she 'made a fortune on crochet hats'. She is now back in Iceland again for the sleep slaughtering season, but she is not very happy there.

'I have decided that Hvammstangi slaughterhouse is not for me, so I am moving on back to Vopnafjörur slaughterhouse where I was previously. There we are allowed to have meat fights, sing and dance and have fun. Hvammstangi was all too modern and serious. Work is about having FUN – nothing else!'

This Norwegian rolling stone is already planning her next step:

'I am probably going to New Zealand in November to meet loads of merino sheep. Just imagine the wonderful crochet hats I can make!' she wrote.

Some years ago, while travelling the ferry from Dover to Calais, I met an unusual English Buddhist named Darren, who was embarking on a journey on foot to a mystical place in the Himalayas, where he felt called to go. The problem with 'Darren, the Buddhist from Gloucester', as I referred to him, was that he went into a complete panic the moment anything went slightly wrong, and that was likely to happen often, for he had a limited comprehension of geography, or where he had to go. Although I spent the afternoon with him and helped him plot out his route across Europe towards Nepal, it is to my regret that I didn't find a way of keeping in touch with him. I would have loved to find out whether he made it to his destination and, more interestingly, what happened to him along the way.

I'm glad I did not make the same mistake with Raggi of Rum.

SEWARD

ANCHORAGE

'The Elf That Got Away'
Kim, the Elf from Vancouver

'The Last Grand Adventure the World Will Ever Have'
Ken Clineman, Park Ranger Extraordinaire, with Jacky

'In Search of the Garbage Dump Bears of Hoonah Island'
Jacky, fooling around with salmon at the Hoonah Salmon Company

'How not to find a Grizzly'
Using the 'Hello Mister Bear' method

'A Bear, a Bus Driver, a Hobbit and a Big ol' Camper Bus'
Getting ready to board

'A Bear, a Bus Driver, a Hobbit and a Big ol' Camper Bus'
Mount Denali, in Denali National Park

'Begging for Chocolate'
Jacky, needing sugar

'Horned Puffins and a Deckhand called Jeff'
Celebrating with salmon, halibut and a toy puffin,
and below, eating our halibut on Homer Spit

'The Blonde Puffins of Resurrection Bay'
Puffin # 8, and Harriet

CHAPTER FIFTY-ONE

Hints for the Happy Traveller

The Moose's Tooth, Anchorage
August 10th — 61°11'25.53"N, 149°52'07.83"W

'The Moose's Tooth' is a well-known, perhaps iconic Alaskan bar, with moose heads on the wall, friendly bartenders and very laid-back customers. Jeans, checked shirts and boots are everywhere to be seen, and my Jack Daniels whiskies are poured to the top!

Spread out before me on the table are my somewhat dog-eared Moleskine notebooks, and I page through them, smiling, remembering, and thinking happy thoughts.

Six weeks ago now, arriving back in Rovaniemi after a week in northern Lapland and Norway, I returned to the B&B I had stayed previously, and the owner welcomed me warmly.

'Ahh, you are back,' she said, 'I remember you from last week.'

As the B&B had been very busy the week before, I was surprised that she remembered me, and I said this to her.

'Bright eyes,' she said, pointing at my face with two fingers stretched apart.

'Excuse me?' I said, not comprehending.

'Happy eyes,' she said, 'you have such happy eyes.'

Indeed, looking back, I think I have had 'happy eyes', even after sleeping on hotel kitchen floors or having long travel delays. As this trip ends, it is helpful to reflect on the reasons for my happy eyes.

Flexibility of travel has been most important for me. Within some boundaries, having the freedom to go and do whatever seems the most interesting has made a big difference. Earlier in this book, I referred to this as finding the place of most potential. My best experiences on this trip have been on the back of having the time and space to spend enough time in each place. This was the case in Greenland where there was no set plan and again in Iceland where we arrived, decided to search for puffins and off we went. When the opportunity to sail across the English Channel on a little yacht arose, I was able to make the time, as I was to visit the Isle of Rum and spend a few days on that most marvellous of islands.

I have done a great deal of travelling on this trip and have used big planes and small planes, buses, trains, trams, tubes, shuttles, bicycles, taxis, rental cars, dog sledges, snowmobiles, ferries, yachts, ships, fishing boats and, much of the time, my own two feet. Many people are put off leaving home by the actual travelling, but unless you see the travelling as part of the experience, I don't recommend the journey!

For example, to reach the Isle of Rum involved two days of travelling on either side of a few days on the island, which seems crazy, but worked out fabulously. I had to catch a flight to Glasgow and a three-hour bus ride to Fort William with an overnight stay at the end. The following day it was a two-hour train ride to a little town called Arisaig, a mile-long hike to the harbour and a lengthy wait for the three-hour ferry to Rum. These journeys turned out to be a fantastic time for me – I listened to music, met interesting people, and got to see the very beautiful Scottish scenery along the way. And then there was Rum.

The interconnectedness of my experiences along the way has also made a big difference. In particular, it has been the animals that have provided the continuity across the countries – the puffins, the bears, the otters, the reindeers and the huskies. People have also kept reappearing on my journey. Santa Claus in Finland and again in Alaska, elves in Finland and Vancouver, Stuart in Greenland and on Rum, Raggi in Greenland and then again, in absentia, in Rum, in Norway and via email, in Alaska.

A changing backing soundtrack has accompanied me along the way, beginning with Irish anthems in Greenland, Scottish tunes on the journey to Rum, trip-hop courtesy of Paul Chung in Finland, jazz in Bermuda and New York, and country music over crab in Alaska.

Here in the Moose's Tooth in Anchorage, country music is king, and as a Paul Brandt song finishes, and Willie Nelson begins, my pizza with all the toppings arrives. An old friend of mine from South Africa, who lived in Anchorage for three months, told me about the Moose's Tooth, and said I should order the 'Hollywood' pizza with everything. I couldn't find that on the menu, but they seemed to understand 'with everything'.

My food choices on this trip have been fairly conventional with a slap-up dinner in Greenland (followed by tinned beans and sausage), haggis and neeps in Scotland, red deer mince in Rum, reindeer sausage and fried up sardines in Finland, iconic New York hotdogs and Alaskan crab and halibut. However, if things had turned out slightly differently, I might have eaten polar bear and seal steaks in Greenland, puffin hearts in Iceland and pony testicles in Rum!

The strange places I visited were made all the stranger by the towns' efforts to promote themselves – from Hammerfest's polar bear pins and most Northerly town tag, to Rovaniemi's Santa Claus Village, to Sonkajarvi's wife-carrying, to Nanaimo's bathtub racing, and to North Pole, Alaska itself, they were all trying to be noticed!

Having a sense of mission when travelling also adds a great deal to the experience. My mission has been to write everyday stories as I found them, but travellers may find their mission in many ways. Some people do this through photographs, or through collecting things along the way, like spoons, thimbles or snow globes. A specific sense of mission can make a trip a lot of fun, particularly when one is not travelling on one's own. Making a movie along the way, where each of you plays different characters and so on, is also great fun. Another type of mission is seeking out something specific, like visiting all the pubs or churches, or finding a particular animal – need I say puffin? Amateur zoology is my favourite, as you might have guessed by now!

On this trip I have tried wherever I can to stay in backpacker lodges, youth hostels or with local families, partly to reduce cost, but more importantly, to meet interesting people. Sitting in one's hotel room and watching television is not the way to experience a foreign country.

Travelling on one's own can be lonely at times, and people cope differently with this challenge. I enjoy having a mix of being on my own and with others, as the shared experience is more fulfilling when I'm with friends, but if I am on my own, I tend to meet more people.

I always have a book nearby, and use the opportunity of delays to sit quietly for a few hours and read, or to meet a few locals. Having pre-booked accommodation on the other side adds to the stress of delays and limits one's ability to improvise while travelling.

All of the above have helped keep my eyes bright and happy these past months.

It is later now, and closing time at The Moose's Tooth. In the morning, I head for home, a new role at work and a new life with Jacky, if she says yes...

I pack my notebooks into my bag, wave to my bartender friend, and make for the door.

CHAPTER FIFTY-TWO

News from Faraway Places

Flying Home
August 11th, 2004 — 56°11'49.91"N, 142°06'35.21"W

This story ends as it began, aboard an aeroplane far from home. My notebooks are nearly full, and with this adventure over I can reflect on lots of new friends, and many interesting people. I've kept in touch with a few of them over email and have had some interesting replies that bring news from faraway places.

On the Isle of Rum itself, life continues at its steady pace, as summer draws to an end, and the cold winds from the Atlantic bring in the autumn and the perfect conditions for picking winkles. Stuart, who was very kind in putting me up and introducing me to Rum from the inside, is still hard at work with Hamish and Harry, the Highland ponies, and that beautiful herd of Highland cows.

Summer is ending in Greenland, the locals are watching for the first signs of ice creep, and the huskies are looking forward to running with the dog sledge again.

My funky friend in Finland, Paul Chung, the happy Korean student travelling the world, sent me a recent update on his travels.

'Dear Rich,' he wrote, 'After Nordkapp, I just go directly to Estonia with eleven hours bus to Rovaniemi and to Helsinki. Overnight train then ferry to Tallinn then bus to my workcamp place. My workcamp over there was okay even though accommodation was a little old, but peoples from France, USA, Australia, Poland and Czech were really great. After that, I went to Sigulda near Riga, capital of Latvia. Sigulda is a national park, and I took some hiking and a one day trip to Riga. Staying at private house at Sigulat at the price of fifteen euro was a great experience even though I couldn't talk with the old lady cuz she can speak only German that I can't speak. But suddenly I felt homesick...then I just passed Lithuania and Poland to Frankfurt with long riding bus of twenty-five hours. Haha. Your book this time was really a companion. I almost read half of it! I want to travel along your route in Aussie and USA in the future with rent car, I hope. Also good chance to know a person called Rich Shapiro. Right now I'm staying at my Korean friend house cooking Korean food feeling like home.'

News from Julia Galvin, the Irish Bog Snorkelling Champion, is that she has finally achieved her dream – winning a world championship.

'Well my friend,' she wrote to me, 'I can proudly say that I am (at last) Ladies Mountain Bike Bog Snorkelling World Champion. It was tough going. I was up against just one other chick. She went in first, in a pair of itty bitty shorts, but it took her a long time to do the event. I did it in 2 minutes, 36 seconds. The bike was filled with lead as was the carrier and basket. I had to wear a lead belt and rucksack. I wore my own trusty snorkel and mask which I think was a help.

I'm back home in the bogs of Kerry for the summer. I've been living a funny old life for a couple of months – me and real life have been eluding each other for so, so long now I don't know what to do with myself.

If I had a bucket of cash I think I would just go around the world doing silly things. In a very strange way, my life is stuck somewhere between a reality and a fantasy. I do things that other people wouldn't even dream of, and I only dream of what other people do.'

I've also had a few emails from Ian Walker, the world's fifth best liar, with kind invitations to visit him in his cold and rainy country and to stay in his barge!

The most recent update from rolling stone Raggi is that the Kulusuk Hotel manager who tried to deny me food and who fired her in Greenland has himself been fired, apparently for drunk driving.

I sent Raggi a few of the stories I wrote for this book, and she replied,

'It's been lovely to read your stories. I smiled a lot where I am sitting in the library in Vopnafjörur in Iceland. I thought the stories were great, and you write in such a way that's easy to follow, and people get a desire to read on and on.'

I've met a lot of other interesting people as well. Tracking down Santa Claus in Lapland and again in Alaska was great fun, as was meeting the 'Admiral' on the trip across the English Channel. There was Bicycle Bobby from England; Ken Clineman, Park Ranger Extraordinaire, in Alaska; Hobbitgirl and the Naked Cowboy from New York City; Walli Mohammed, the Bermudan taxi driver and jazz expert; Erin McLarnon, the dog musher from Anchorage; the goat girls of Na Hearadh, and, of course, Mister Johnny Barnes, the statue who gave me a ride.

He'd had such a simple message:

'If every individual in this world, he'd said to me, could just do one thing to make another person happy, just one thing, imagine what a difference that would make.'
Imagine.

As I shook his hand one last time, he looked me in the eye and said again, ' Just one thing '

HOME sweet HOME

A few more photographs...

'When the Isle of Rum comes to Greenland'
Rich on Mt. Rich

'Balls to the Wall'
Ally the deerstalker (left), Stuart and Sean in front, and Chris (James Herriot) telling
his stories. In the far right background is Ed, Rum Reserve Manager

'The Home of the Original Job'
Stuart and two of his Rum ponies

'The Goat Girls of Na Hearadh'
Isle of Rum Storekeeper, Kate and her sister, Roz, Goat Girl No. 2

'Interviewing Claus'
Pete, the amorous elf

'The World's Fifth Best Liar'
Sarah and Ian before the big race

'The Statue Who Gave Me a Ride'
Mister Johnny Barnes and Rich on Crow Lane roundabout,
and below, Johnny calling us over

'Anybody can be Santa'
Jacky and Santa at North Pole, Alaska

'Fourteen Years'
Love and presents
(Photo taken in the carpark of Santa Claus House,
North Pole, Alaska, August 1st, 2004)

CHAPTER FIFTY-THREE

Fourteen Years

August 11th, 2018 — 51°22'17.86"N, 0°27'28.45"W

The Moleskine journals have stood silent now for fourteen years, lined up in a neat, black row on a shelf, glaring at me as my best of intentions were distracted by life. Trapped inside, the stories you've read were waiting to be shared, and in the waiting, the people in the stories have moved on to new adventures.

Raggi of Rum, the rolling stone, did end up gathering her own moss, and is now living in a remote part of Norway with *'four kids, a man, a house, two cars, a snowmobile and a steady job! Hehe, what happened?'* she writes, still laughing at the world.

Stuart Shaw, the 'keeper of the cows' on Rum, still works for Scottish Natural Heritage, but on the mainland, not too far away from Rum.

The Isle of Rum is still there for you to discover, and new generations of goat girls, deerstalkers, rat-catchers and winkle-pickers would be happy to meet you, I'm sure. Accommodation ranges from a guest house to the community bunkhouse! I reached out to the Rum team and was delighted to hear that Hamish and Harry, my two favourite ponies, are still alive and doing well. Old age has turned Harry completely white!

The goat girls have also moved on, but not that far, for Lesley is now the Reserve Manager of Rum, and is actively involved in all aspects of island life. This includes monitoring the growing population of Manx Shearwaters (puffinus puffinus), and she tells me that the cold winters are helping keep the rats in check!

Her fellow goat girl, Roz, has a doctorate in Ecology, and lectures biology at West College Scotland in Glasgow. After leaving Rum, Roz worked in Kielder Forest, Northumberland, where she researched the disease dynamics of wild rodent populations. She later moved to Cork, Ireland, where she completed her PhD on the effects of grazing management on the biodiversity of the Irish uplands. *'I'm still good friends with Lesley, and we meet up several times a year,'* Roz writes.

Dr Ian Walker, the world's fifth best liar, teaches statistics and traffic psychology at the University of Bath, and in his spare time does ultra-endurance events. This year he competed in the 4200 km cycle race from Italy to Nordkapp, where Paul Chung and I stood looking out over the Arctic Ocean towards the North Pole, all those years ago.

Speaking of Paul, we've lost contact, and despite my best efforts via social media and other means, I haven't been able to find him. My eleven-year-old daughter, Kate, says I should go to Seoul and walk the streets calling his name. I like to think he's in the music travelling business, if there is such a thing, for he was so well-suited to that. Come to think of it; I never did understand the trip-hop genre that was his favourite. Maybe he was the real guy behind *Gangnam Style*, or perhaps there's a roaming campervan out there, beating out badman ballads, full of small children with surprised hair styles. Paul, if you're out there, find <u>me</u>!

Of all of us, Julia Galvin, the Ladies Mountain Bike Bog Snorkelling World Champion, is still living the dream. She continued to participate in the Wife-Carrying and the Bog Snorkelling for many years and, in between, has done Christmas tree throwing contests and the World Stone Throwing Competition. She lives in Listowel in County Kerry, Ireland. Dame Julia, as you should refer to her, is now actually Dame Commander of the Serene Order of Leonard, from the Principality of Hutt River. The latter is a tiny area within Australia, about 600km north of Perth, which claims to have seceded from Australia and formed their own micro-nation. Julia contacted HRH Prince Leonard in 2008 expressing an interest in becoming their representative in select sporting events, and given her status as a world champion, they granted her citizenship, and she became their global novelty sports representative, and they made her a 'Dame'. She even undertook a formal visit to the micro-nation and in their chapel, knelt before royalty, and had the sword duly applied to both shoulders.

Mister Johnny Barnes, 'the statue who gave me a ride', finally retired from his stint at Crow Lane roundabout in Bermuda, in December 2015. He passed away six months later at the age of 93, having imparted love and friendship to thousands. His place on the roundabout was taken up by Dennis Bean, and you can visit him there yourself, near to Johnny's statue.

Erin McLarnon, the dog musher, still lives in Willow, Alaska, about 65 miles north of Anchorage, where she and her husband, Paul, run Broken Runner Sled Dog Kennel, and care for between 40 and 60 dogs that are too old to race anymore.

Santa Claus continues his normal routine, in the forest outside Rovaniemi in Finland and also in North Pole, Alaska. He still visits me every year. If you would like to write to him, his address is P.O. Box 1, Lapland, Finland. His elf, Pete, however, has disappeared, and it is entirely probable that he is still chasing girls, or possibly boys, one country at a time.

The puffins, polar bears and many species globally have been impacted by global warming, over-fishing, deforestation and much more, and need all the support we can provide, whether it is financial, educational, or signing up to be a goat girl, rat man or insect girl!

I contacted the Alaska SeaLife Center in Seward to find out what happened to my puffins, and whether any were still alive. In a surreal moment, I opened an email from Kristen, their Assistant Avian Curator (Puffingirl's correct title) to hear that five of my six puffins were still alive, with Trailer Trash and Fabio, who were really old when I saw them, still going! She wrote:

'Trailer and Fabio are still here, and at 32 years, are now some of the oldest tufted puffins in any alcid aviary. Trailer is fairly blind now, and Fabio only has one good eye.'

She added that when Trailer started having vision problems, Fabio 'acted as her seeing eye puffin, showing her around habitat and calling to her so she wouldn't get lost. It was very sweet. Fabio still grows the longest tufts of any puffin, even in his old age.'

Of the two tufted puffins shown in the photograph in this book, Puffin # 8 (who was called Casanova, according to Kristen) has passed away, and Harriet found a new mate in Antonio and successfully bred with him.

Kristen wrote, 'Harriet is still our sassiest tufted puffin'.

The summer of 2004 was the summer of my life, an amazing period of nonchalance and spontaneity, where the next friend was only a conversation away. It gave me time to show deep interest in people and be part of their personal stories. It allowed my sense of humour to embrace and ride with the ridiculous at times, and it took me to places without guidebooks. It showed me nature in all its splendour and gave me reverence for the world around me. And at the end of it all, perhaps because of it all, at a faraway place called Wonder Lake in Alaska, I begged for chocolate and found love.

Jacky did say yes and we were married the following year, with Robbo, my fellow puffin conspirator, as master of ceremonies. We have three beautiful daughters, Kate (11), Annie (9) and Rosie (5). They adore animals of every kind, and use any opportunity to get close to them, with little regard for personal safety! Perhaps my being an amateur zoologist has rubbed off on them? We live in Surrey, England, although we keep close links with South Africa and visit often.

As a side note, to show that my frolic with poor planning has not been entirely lost, last year we took the girls to the Faroe Islands, a remote island grouping somewhere between the UK and Iceland. I wanted to show them cliffs filled with puffins, and we hiked to the top of a huge cliff and peered over at thousands of empty nest sites. The puffins had all left for the winter just the week before!

My day job as a partner in a big four accounting firm in London sees me lead a technology platform that maps data onto the world map, and helps clients make better decisions about the world. There is some irony that I find myself, as the free-spirited traveller, insisting that clients don't make the same mistakes, and go unprepared into the big, wonderful world!

Reading these stories again takes me back immediately to the windswept green hills of Rum, the howling huskies of Greenland and the far-off plains of Alaska, where a green camper bus waits for me to board.

What are you doing next summer?

Reading these stories again takes me back immediately to the windswept green hills of Rum, the howling huskies of Greenland and the far-off plains of Alaska, where a green camper bus waits for me to board.

What are you doing next summer?

Postscript on the Puffins

It could be said that this book has been about people, places and puffins, with puffins being the collective term for the many beautiful animals I encountered on this journey. It was, however, the puffin that caught my imagination the most. In learning about these 'clowns of the sea' I also better appreciated the need for conservation, and gained new respect for all those involved in these efforts.

At the time of completing this book, puffins are in decline globally, with the Atlantic puffin now listed as a vulnerable species. Birdlife International has several projects that help the puffin and other seabirds. These include their work on gillnet fishing by-catch in Japan, which are a threat to both the Tufted and Horned Puffins in winter, the eradication of rats on seabird breeding islands in the Atlantic and their work to advocate more protected areas globally.

As a way of completing my own journey, I have committed to donate the proceeds from the sale of this book to Birdlife International, to support their work in the conservation of puffins and other seabirds around the world, and I hope for my family and me to be personally involved in some of these projects. Perhaps this will also inspire my own daughters to follow in the footsteps of the goat girls, and help preserve our beautiful planet.

Rich

October 2018

References

Darwin, Charles. On the Origin of Species. 6th Edition. Amazon Books

Lonely Planet Publications. Bermuda: A Lonely Planet Survival Kit. Hawthorn, Australia: Lonely Planet Publications

Michener, J, 1988. Alaska. New York: Ballantine Books

Netid Publications. The Visitor's Guide to Iceland. Reykjavik: Netid Publications

Nicolson, Adam. The Seabird's Cry. London. William Collins

Rough Guides Ltd. The Rough Guide to Alaska. London: Penguin Books

Scottish Natural Heritage, Rum: Kinloch Castle. Perth, Scotland: SNH Publications

Scottish Natural Heritage, Rum: Nature's Island, Perth, Scotland: SNH Publications

Steel, T, 1994. The Life and Death of St. Kilda. London: HarperCollins

Thordasen, T. Classic Geology in Europe 3: Iceland. 2nd Edition. London. Dunedin Academic Press

About the author

Rich Shapiro is an enthusiastic traveller who likes to take sabbaticals from his day job. He immerses himself in the people and places he visits, and enjoys putting himself in 'the place of most opportunity'. Rich records these stories by hand in Moleskine notebooks, and this book is the story of one such sabbatical – around and about the Arctic Circle. Rich is now married to Jacky, the girlfriend in the latter part of this book, and they have three daughters, Kate, Annie and Rosie.

Also by Rich Shapiro

Losing Sight of the Shore (2003)
Belinda, the brave and inspiring story of the girl who never gave up, by Belinda Walton (2011) (editing role)

' I have to use the piggy back method,' Julia had said (179) to me earlier, ' Otherwise I just slide off at an angle - I'm a bit top heavy,' she had laughed.

'So do puffins have divorces then?' I echoed purplehead.

'Excuse me?' He looked at me strangely.

' Do puffins have divorces?' I asked again,' You know, so they know when to get lost?'

Puffins are monogamous and mate for life. However they are only together for 4-6 weeks each year, at the nesting site. For the rest of the year they are at sea, in large groups, or alone.

    The Wife Carrying World Championships, Sonkajar
    The Irish Bog Snorkelling Champion, Sonkajarvi,
    Fame on a Sunday Morning, Iisalmi, Finland, :
    The World's Fifth Best Liar, Helsinki, Finland,
    Into the Land of Pink, Hamilton, Bermuda, :
    The Rare Bermudian Sea Otter, Shelly Bay, J
    The Statue Who Gave Me a Ride, Barnes Corner

The Virgin Sailor, Ouistreham Yacht Harbour, Normand
Bicycle Bobby, Bayeux, Normandy, France, ...
That Beach called Omaha, Omaha Beach, Norm
A Message from my Hoover, Fort William, Scotland
Balls to the Wall, The Isle of Rum, Scotland,
Rum or Ruin Kinloch, The Isle of Rum, J
the House of the Magical Job, The Isle of Rum, :
The Goat Girls of the Heredith, On the train from R
The Forbidden Isle, Kinloch Castle, The Isle of Rum
Puffins in their Porridge, Glasgow, Scotland, I...
Christmas in June, Santa's Village, Lapland, J...
A Midsummer Day Dream, Rovaniemi, Lapland, J
A New Friend, Kaamanen, Lapland, June ...

Siggy, un-loudlady, said ' Puffins - oh I know when & you'll find them ...'

The puffin, according to the photograph in the tourist shop, is a small chubby white bird, with black wings and a black neck, and a large, orange black orange beak. 10 m of them live in Iceland in the summer, more than anywhere else in the world. They are famous. If you come to Iceland, you just have to see them.

It was no contest really. Pille grabbed his rifle, resting it on the snow in front of him, and with a boom that I think is still travelling across some distant ice floe on the Arctic Circle, fired a bullet through its brain.

Hifi set
Clothing
Stationery
Rifles
Fishing
Fast Food
Apples
Cash out
Toys
Baked beans   Modern Technology
T-bones   What is your wife like?
Seal biltong   Any children?
No english
Post office
Postcards   All the colours.
Hardware
Powdered milk   I love 'em all.
White eggs
(free range?)   Wiggle Wiggle - Ha Ha

Bottle store   Guilty ...
Tobacconist   The Kinloch Trading Store
Gift shop

They said to me, "We're going to build a statue of me." I said to them ' Don't do it while I'm alive. When I die it is too late to approach it ...'

Craftsman
Winkle picklers
Butcher to banisters
Tour guide